On the Same Track

How Schools Can Join the
Twenty-First-Century Struggle
Against Resegregation

Carol Corbett Burris

A Simmons College/Beacon Press
Race, Education, and Democracy Series Book

BEACON PRESS
BOSTON

Beacon Press
Boston, Massachusetts
www.beacon.org

Beacon Press books
are published under the auspices of
the Unitarian Universalist Association of Congregations.

This book is published as part of the Simmons College/Beacon Press
Race, Education, and Democracy Lecture and Book Series and is based
on lectures delivered at Simmons College in 2012.

17   16   15   14   8   7   6   5   4   3   2   1

This book is printed on acid-free paper that meets the uncoated paper
ANSI/NISO specifications for permanence as revised in 1992.

Text design and composition by Wilsted & Taylor Publishing Services

Library of Congress Cataloging-in-Publication Data

Burris, Carol Corbett.
  On the same track : how schools can join the twenty-first-century struggle against
resegregation / Carol Corbett Burris.
      pages cm. — (A Simmons College/Beacon Press race, education, and democracy
series book)
  Includes bibliographical references and index.
  ISBN 978-0-8070-3297-8 (hardback)
  1. Track system (Education)—United States. 2. Educational equalization—United
States. I. Title.
  LB3061.8.B88 2013
  371.2'540973—dc23   2013039594

To my granddaughter, Maxine.
>   May the schools you attend be excellent
>   for you and for every child.

To my husband, Jesse,
>   whose support, guidance, and feedback
>   were so important to the writing of this book.

To Kevin Welner and Jeannie Oakes,
>   whose research, teachings, and mentorship
>   helped me understand the complexities of tracking.

And to Bill Johnson,
>   whose courage, guidance, and political savvy
>   allowed us to do the right thing
>   by all of Rockville Centre's children.

Contents

Introduction

When I first sat down to write this book, I was conflicted. What more was there to say about tracking? So much research has accumulated across the decades on how tracking stratifies our schools by race and class. Countless studies have shown its depressive effect on the achievement of students in low-track classes. Sociologists have done an excellent job explaining the factors and beliefs that support its continuance, describing in detail the way that prejudice, power, and privilege keep it in place. What relevance would a book about a practice that has been around since the beginning of the twentieth century have for educators and parents of the twenty-first century?

The more I thought about it, however, the more convinced I became that what we have learned from studying tracking can and must inform our views of what is happening in schools today. The beliefs and assumptions that support tracking are the same beliefs and assumptions that are driving current school-reform efforts. The sorting of students by test scores, school-choice policies that result in racially stratified schools, and the abandonment of integration in favor of highly segregated charter schools threaten to take us back to the days of "separate but equal" education.

Every book is born in time, and this book is no exception. I wrote it during the most tumultuous period for public schooling I can remember. Indeed, many public school educators and education researchers wonder if public schooling as we know it will survive the latest wave of reform.

This turmoil has occurred because the leadership for school reform has shifted from educators and schools of education to the private sector and politicians. By financing think tanks and advocacy groups, America's financial elite, including Michael Bloomberg, Bill Gates, Eli Broad, and the Walton family, now have a more powerful influence on state and national education policy than do district superintendents, teachers, and education researchers. Private sector investors have made vast fortunes in the marketplace, and it is the ideas and values of the marketplace that they bring to education reform.

The two buzzwords most often associated with twenty-first-century reform are *accountability* and *choice*. Accountability is measured by student test results. Choice is realized through school-voucher programs, charter schools, application processes, admissions testing ("test-in" schooling), and lotteries. They work hand in hand. School quality is determined by student test scores, which in turn drive the parental decision-making process. Teachers are evaluated based on test scores and sorted into groups for censure, possible dismissal, and reward. The belief of contemporary marketplace reformers is that eventually the free market will ensure that only excellent schools and excellent teachers survive. Like tracking, market-based reforms are a sort-and-select system.

But will sorting and selecting make our schools better? No reasonable educator would argue that test scores should be ignored or that school and teacher quality do not matter. However, an unintended consequence of choice policies is that some children are left behind—the ones who do not make the score cut and are retained in their grade, the ones whose parents do not have the time or resources to make an informed choice.

And what happens to the neighborhood school that is not chosen? As high achievers move out of a school, school achievement plummets and the school begins a downward spiral, often leading to eventual closure and the displacement of students. If teachers and principals are evaluated by means of student test scores, where will they be incentivized to teach and to lead—in struggling schools, or in those schools with a proven track record of success?

If we pause for a moment and look at the research literature, we will find the answers to these questions. We already know what occurs when students are sorted and grouped for instruction by the practice known as tracking. As school-choice policies are implemented, entire schools become tracks by virtue of selective entrance policies and segregated neighborhoods. We are now engaging in tracking writ large, based on the misguided belief that competition is fair and that it will improve our schools. We have absolutely no evidence to indicate that either assumption is true, but nevertheless, politicians and policymakers forge ahead.

In this book I argue that the impulse to sort and select students (and schools) and put them on separate trajectories is one of the foremost contributors to the achievement gaps found in our public schools today. Indeed, I will argue that if we are ever to accomplish what we hope to accomplish—true school reform that addresses the needs of *all* children—we will have to stop the sorting of students and build strong, diverse schools and classrooms.

The effects of sorting are clear when it comes to race and socioeconomic status. Study after study has shown that in schools, as in districts with diverse student populations, tracking results in racial stratification and lower achievement in low-track classes. In both integrated and single-race schools it results in socioeconomic stratification as well. Indeed, one of the arguments I will make in this book is that racial and class prejudice propels the creation of sorting systems and sustains their continuance. This was true in the 1980s, when education scholar Jeannie Oakes began her research on tracking, and it is true today.[1] History tells us that separate is not equal. The effects of detracking are equally clear: when all students are given the highest levels of instruction, all rise to the challenge.

In the first part of this book (chapters 1–4), I will review what we know about sorting students into tracks. I will discuss the ways in which educators have attempted to make tracking work and the problems inherent in such attempts. I will show how the sorting of students affects the composition of classrooms, and how it affects student achievement. I will also discuss the beliefs and prejudices that sustain tracking and other sort-and-select policies.

The second part of the book looks at the experiences of schools that have implemented or attempted to implement detracking reforms. Some have made tremendous progress; others have realized incremental gains. One chapter profiles the Rockville Centre, New York, high school in which I serve as principal. The school realized significant benefits when it began giving all students access to the best curriculum in detracked classrooms.

Detracking efforts are not without challenges. Detracking is a difficult reform to enact because it meets with tremendous resistance from those who receive (or believe they receive) benefit from tracking. Such resistance can be overcome, however, and strategies on meeting this challenge are also presented herein.

Finally, this book will discuss how what we know about tracking can and should inform our present path of education reform. In moving ahead, caution is warranted, for the deleterious effects of sorting students are already emerging as unintended consequences of today's market-based reforms. The stated goal of today's reformers is to make all students ready for college and career. It is a noble goal, worthy of our embrace. However, it is a goal that can quickly devolve from "college *and* career readiness" to "college *or* career readiness"—with students being sorted into life paths as a result of policies that lead to greater inequities of opportunity. Unless sorting and selecting in all its forms is addressed, such a devolution is inevitable. This book is my attempt to help ensure it does not occur.

I

The Boy with the Purple Tie

During the spring of 2012 I read an article that appeared in the British newspaper the *Guardian* titled "School Colour-Codes Pupils by Ability."[1] Accompanying the story was a photograph of three smiling, handsome boys wearing school uniforms: blazers and ties. The boy on the left wears a blue tie; the boy on the right, a red one. The young man in the center sports a purple tie. He is literally head and shoulders above the other two. According to the article, the color of the boy's tie distinguishes him as a gifted and talented student.

The school profiled in the article is Crown Woods College, in the Greenwich district of London. At Crown Woods, students are sorted into three ability levels and assigned to separate buildings, buildings that, like the students' uniforms, are color-coded. Students from the three buildings eat lunch at different times, and their play areas are separated by fences.

The physical separation of students at Crown Woods begins at age eleven. Each pupil is ranked at the end of primary school, and this ranking determines which of the three buildings, or "houses," on the

Crown Woods site they will attend. Michael Murphy, the headmaster, has credited the "small schools" model of the United States as the origin of his idea to put three "mini-schools"—Delamere, Ashwood, and Sherwood—on one site. Delamere is reserved for the gifted and talented; its students wear purple badges on their blazers. The other two schools—Ashwood and Sherwood—are mixed-achievement, but students are "streamed," according to ability, into three levels within the building. Ashwood students wear blue badges and Sherwood students wear red. According to Michael Murphy, streaming "is the only way to survive in the brave new world of market-driven education."[2] Apparently, parents are banging down the doors in order that their children be given the chance to wear purple.

The belief that the most effective way to educate students is to group them by "ability" is hardly a new concept, and in an age of market-based reform, it's entirely possible that a school of purple ties is coming to a neighborhood near you—if it hasn't already. Purple ties, seen and unseen, have been with us for a very long time thanks to the process of sorting and selecting known as tracking. The purple tie can be seen as a symbol of the elitist impulses that too often result in inequitable practices and uneven access to excellence. The funneling of students into ability-based mini-schools, along with a similar stratification occurring within schools, is clearly an example of tracking on a grand scale.

In an education context, *tracking* has a number of meanings. Some researchers use the term to refer to systems that keep students together across the curriculum. This was the case during the first half of the twentieth century, when students were assigned to college-prep, general, or vocational tracks with no allowance for movement between tracks. For the most part, these systems have been dismantled and replaced by systems of curriculum differentiation, where course offerings reflect various levels of difficulty and students are placed in them based on their aptitude as measured by testing, or they are required to meet certain prerequisites.[3] This practice is often referred to as "ability grouping." For example, students might be assigned to different levels of the same course or to a course with a separate curriculum that is either more or less rigorous.[4]

Other synonyms of *tracking* include *leveling*, a word that suggests a more flexible and equitable system, and *streaming*, which is the term generally used in Great Britain. No matter what term is used, however, if you educate one group of students apart from another as a way to address perceived differences in ability, you are tracking. For clarity and simplicity, *tracking* will be the term used in this book to describe all such grouping configurations. My definition of the practice as it occurs today is as follows:

> Tracking is the sorting of students within a school or district that results in different access to academic curriculum and the opportunity to learn.

The addition of the word *district* in the definition is important. Think about our purple-tie example. In that case, the track was a school within a group of schools. Tracking can occur within a classroom, within a grade level, within a school, or even within a school system. For example, school-choice systems in which test results or other criteria determine admission is a form of within-district tracking. Although this book will focus primarily on within-school tracking, from time to time it will discuss how the characteristics of tracking play out on a wider scale, especially in large districts. This is important because, across the country, sorting students into schools by means of selection policies is on the rise.

ORIGINS OF TRACKING

Tracking was not always a part of American public schooling. It began at the start of the last century during what is commonly referred to as the Progressive Era, when schools were asked to address the social and economic concerns attendant upon the influx of immigrants from southern and eastern Europe.[5] The "cult of efficiency" made it imperative for immigrant children to learn English along with American cultural and societal mores. At the same time, the upwardly mobile native-born, as well as the upper class, wanted their children to have a challenging, college-preparatory education uncompromised by the presence of immigrant students in their classes. Social Darwinism and the scientific measurement of intelligence by IQ tests were prevalent belief systems at the time.[6]

Sort-and-select policies were embraced by administrative progressives as an efficient and scientific way to school students according to their academic capacity, social class, and future life stations. Educator Leonard Ayres, author of *Laggards in Our Schools* (1909), argued that schools were designed for intelligent students and special programs were needed for the majority, who were making unacceptably slow progress.[7] The idea that schools must prepare citizens for their predicted stations in life was echoed in the National Education Association report "Cardinal Principles of Secondary Education of 1918."[8] The purpose of high school was to support democracy, and the purpose of democracy was "to so organize society that each member may develop his personality primarily through activities designed for the well-being of his fellow members and of society as a whole."[9] It is within this historical context that tracking began. In short, tracking was an attempt by schools to create a differentiated curriculum in order to prepare a diverse population for a range of societal needs.[10]

That racial and class stratification resulted from tracking became quickly apparent, but early critiques of the practice fell on deaf ears. From the 1930s through the 1950s, girls, minorities, immigrants, and students from low-income households were routinely placed into nonacademic tracks.[11] Tracking was not seriously analyzed until the middle of the twentieth century, when researchers questioned how the practice replicated the hierarchical social order, thus inhibiting social progress through public education.

QUESTIONS RAISED BY RESEARCHERS

In 1959 the sociologist Talcott Parsons, in "The School Class as a Social System," published in the *Harvard Educational Review*, identified "curriculum differentiation" as an important in-school factor in the sorting and selecting of youth for their future roles in society.[12] The research community realized that school tracking must be included as a factor when considering student outcomes, as well as when measuring the effects of schools on American society and social progress. Researchers began to ask important questions: To what extent does school tracking perpetuate the established hierarchy of society at large? Is high-track (college prep) placement fairly distributed (based on merit only) or do class and race affect track placement? Do students and their families understand the long-term implications of track placement?

It quickly became apparent that something was terribly amiss. More students expressed interest in attending college than were actually given access to the college track, often resulting in student confusion when those who believed their public school education was preparing them for college found this not to be the case. The college-preparatory track was in fact considered by schools to be a scarce resource, and only a limited number of students were given access.[13] It thus became important for researchers to understand the mechanisms schools used to put students into these life-determining tracks. If college-track assignment was both desirable and limited, access to that track should be based on merit, and entrance criteria should not reflect racial or class bias.

It had generally been believed that academic ability was the deciding factor in track placement, with other factors, such as socioeconomic status, making small contributions. To see if that was the case, researchers weighed the parents' education levels, occupations, and the number of books in the home to create a formula used to determine the effects of social status on track placement.[14] Using this formula, they found that social status trumped ability in determining the greatest effect on track placement. This led to the conclusion that "curriculum differentiation may indeed serve as an important mechanism for maintaining status advantages through the educational system."[15]

It appeared, then, that tracking gave the advantage to students from homes with higher social status. That advantage was compounded because students in high-track classes benefited from contact with higher-status peers, who had higher expectations for continuing their education. Other researchers, who saw track placement as primarily a result of test scores, questioned whether test scores should be the primary determinant of track placement.[16]

By the 1970s, researchers concluded that incentives for student performance, such as high grades, were not equally distributed among the tracks. The academic potential and performance of lower-track students was undervalued as compared with students in the upper tracks, where student achievement was recognized and rewarded. Education researcher Barbara Heyns was one of the first to identify tracking as a contributor to status advantage and disadvantage, both within the school and in the larger community.[17] According to Heyns, tracking contributed to social stratification in society at large. Segregating students within schools creates an academic hierarchy that results in different access to school resources.

An understanding was emerging that track placement was not a neutral way to deliver instruction but rather a "socially significant classification" that shapes the way the school community and eventually the larger society responds to a student.[18] Researchers, in short, were learning that tracking put young people on a life path from which it was difficult to veer or exit. As noted earlier, this was occurring without students or their families understanding the implications. Tracking made "students less able to anticipate the frustration of their educational plans."[19] In other words, students thought that they were on the path to upward mobility by being prepared for college when, sadly, they were not. Tracking and its implications with respect to student achievement, opportunities to learn, self-esteem, and later success became a topic of further interest for researchers.

INVOLVEMENT OF THE COURTS

The way tracking was racially stratifying classrooms was not lost on those who studied it in the 1960s and '70s, nor was it lost on the courts. After the Supreme Court's 1954 decision in *Brown v. Board of Education*, judges took a hard look at tracking as a form of "second generation" segregation, finding that tracking was being used to re-segregate African American students in integrated schools. Even if the intent was not explicit or deliberate, the practice had the effect of producing segregation at the classroom level.[20]

In a 1967 court decision, *Hobson v. Hansen*, Judge James Skelly Wright ruled that the *Brown* decree banning school segregation also applied to de facto segregation in the schools of the District of Columbia, and that the use of IQ scores to track students in the DC schools was discriminatory.[21] After establishing the strong correlation between race and class and track assignment, the judge ruled that

> when state imposed classifications dealing with critical person rights—as [Judge Wright] ruled education to be—operated in a way that placed the heaviest burdens on the poor and culturally disadvantaged—as assignment to lower tracks seemed to—"then the state had to come forward and show a compelling reason for proceeding as they did."[22]

During the trial, the defendant, DC Superintendent of Schools Carl Hansen, offered the IQ test as the basis for track decisions. Of great interest to the court was how inflexible the system was and that the test had been standardized on a sample of students who were white and middle class. The judge concluded that the test was a measure of social class, not ability. He ruled that the IQ tests used to track students were culturally biased because they were standardized on a white, middle-class sample and, therefore, not appropriate for the assignment of poor black children to ability groups. The court abolished the tracking system used in the District of Columbia. On appeal, the tracking system was reinstated, but the district was forbidden to use IQ tests as the basis for track assignment.

In a 1970 paper in the Harvard publication *Inequality in Education*, researcher Em Hall confirmed the DC court's finding that track placement had as much to do with a student's race and class as any academic factor and that tracking tended to "harden the race and class lines drawn in the larger society."[23]

According to Hall, there are three key questions a court must ask when reviewing tracking policies: One, do low-track compensatory programs actually result in greater opportunity later on? (that is, does remediation work so that students eventually move to higher-track classes?) Two, does the system have a rational means by which it selects students for track placement, ensuring that the system is fair? Three, and most important, does tracking work as an educational strategy to increase student learning? Hall's questions would emerge over and over again as researchers examined tracking in the next decades.

The court's concerns regarding tracking were shared by the civil rights community. In 1976 the US Commission on Civil Rights issued a report that evaluated school desegregation efforts.[24] The commission referred to ability grouping as "the most common cause of classroom segregation," finding that it created racially identifiable classrooms in desegregated schools and that the proportion of minority students in low-track classes rose as the percentage of minority students in the school increased.[25] According to the report, some districts had to go so far as to prohibit the formation of single-race classes.

In the 1980s, as part of an extensive report on desegregation,

Janet Eyler and her colleagues documented the effects of school policies that result in resegregation.[26] The first practice they examined
was ability grouping in the lower grades. The authors' review of the
literature found that, one, students of color and poverty were more
likely to be assigned to low-track classes; two, tracks were rigid, with
very little student movement between them; three, less time was
spent on instruction in low-track classes; and four, there was little
evidence that instruction was tailored to the ability group.

Likewise, Eyler and her colleagues found that tracking at the high
school level produced racially identifiable track levels, with minority students overrepresented in low-track and vocational-track classes
and underrepresented in classes designed for the college bound. They
described the effects of tracking as "cumulative," with students in low
tracks falling further and further behind. They also noted that the
more racially balanced the school, the greater the resegregation in
the classrooms.

MOVEMENT TOWARD REFORM

By the 1980s, tracking could no longer be seen as an equity-neutral
education structure. That children of color were consigned to lower-
ability classes was obvious to anyone who had ever taught or visited
a racially mixed school. Tracking identified students in a public way
based on their capacity to learn *as determined by school officials*. The
labeling affected how students thought of themselves, how they were
perceived by peers, and how seriously their teachers took their learning potential. Debate surrounding the effectiveness and equity of
tracking systems would rage for decades as tracking moved from the
rigid, inflexible systems of the early twentieth century to the various
forms of curricular stratification that exist in schools today.

However, the changes in the tracking system did not happen
by chance. A great deal of the credit for how our understanding of

tracking has evolved, and for the movement toward democratic reform of tracking practices, belongs to a remarkable educator. In 1980 Jeannie Oakes received her PhD from the University of California at Los Angeles. Oakes's dissertation would form the basis of the most important work on the subject of tracking, a book recommended as a must-read by the American School Board's journal.[27] Oakes's *Keeping Track: How Schools Structure Inequality*, published in 1985, would forever change how schools thought about the sorting of students.

2

Keeping Track

Challenging the Status Quo on Grouping Practices

In the 1970s, Jeannie Oakes was an English teacher in a suburban California district. She vividly remembers her first day teaching middle school students. She had four preparations—a music class, two honors English classes, a regular-track English class, and a class called Basic English. Basic English was sixth period—as any teacher knows, a time of day when middle school students tend to be antsy and easily distracted. On that first day of class, she recalls her students looking around the room and saying, "This is the dumb class." Even though they came from seven different elementary schools, they knew enough about each other to know that they had been placed in the school's lowest track.

No matter how hard she worked, or how well she planned, Oakes could not overcome the anti-school culture of the Basic English class. Students were apathetic on a good day and disruptive on a bad one. "During my first year, I could not figure out how I could be so good in the morning, and so bad in the afternoon," she recalled in a recent interview.[1] She gradually became convinced that it was not her teaching, nor was it her students. It was the tracking structure in place in the school that was producing such wildly different results in her various classrooms.

Oakes was one of fourteen young and idealistic teachers who had been hired that year. The following year, she talked her colleagues into abandoning the school's tracking system and instituting heterogeneous classrooms, where children that had previously been grouped by "ability" now learned together. Not only was the new grouping structure successful, her colleagues loved it. The students were more engaged in learning, and the traditional low-track students improved in terms of both behavior and academic performance. Oakes continued to think about the effects of tracking during the summer months when she taught a special program for gifted students. She quickly realized that the activities she was doing with the students who were labeled gifted were activities that would benefit all students, and she worked to make the program more inclusive.

After four years in the middle school, Oakes moved to the district high school, where an entrenched tracking system was in place. The teachers were excellent and highly skilled, but unlike her idealistic middle-school colleagues, they were very set in their ways. In addition, her nontraditional ideas about curriculum and learning were not well received by the school's administration. Oakes decided it was time for a change, and she left teaching to enter UCLA's doctoral program, where she had the opportunity to work with one of education's giants—John Goodlad.

At the time, Goodlad was engaged in a massive research project that would lead to what many consider his most important work—an insightful and comprehensive study of American schooling titled *A Place Called School*.[2] Oakes was intrigued with his ideas regarding multiage grouping as an alternative to tracking, and she became his student and a researcher on his team.

Gathering data for the study was daunting. Goodlad and his team studied thousands of classrooms in seven states representing different regions of the United States. In each state, the team studied two districts that included at least one elementary, middle, and high school. They collected their data from structured interviews of teachers, parents, principals, and students, as well as survey questionnaires and classroom observations. Because the course names and levels were included in the data set, it was a unique opportunity for Oakes to look at a huge amount of data through the lens of tracking.

As she carefully pored through the data, she saw, in school after school across the United States, the replication of her own experiences teaching tracked classes. In her dissertation and a 1980 paper, Oakes first shared her conclusions.[3] What she discovered in her research with Goodlad would form the basis of her award-winning book, *Keeping Track*.[4]

TRACK PLACEMENT AND LEARNING VARIANCES

Comparing high- and low-track classes, Oakes found that there were notable differences in both the quantity of learning, the topics learned, the cognitive skills required of students, and the level and quality of student participation and interaction. Tellingly, student descriptions of their learning differed markedly depending on their track placement. Children in low-track classes, for example, reported learning "how to blow up light bulbs"; "nothing"; "that English is boring"; "only my Roman numerals." Students in high-track classes reported that they learned "how to do what scientists do"; "how to read a classic novel"; and "how to do research in a college library."[5] Oakes found that

> students in low-track classes were most likely to be exposed to topics which emphasize basic literacy skills or life or work oriented instruction, such as filling out forms. These students

were most likely to be engaged in instructional activities which require only lower level cognitive processes—rote learning, comprehension and application. They were not likely to be required to evaluate or think critically. Additionally, teachers of low-track classes who had general behaviors as learning goals for their students most often emphasized student conformity—punctuality, working quietly, and following rules or outlined class procedures.[6]

In contrast, students in high-track classes engaged in higher-level thinking and more cognitively engaging tasks. The results of both survey and observational data clearly indicated that students in high-track classes had more instructional time (as opposed to time spent on routines and behavior management), and the expectations for time spent on homework were higher. Further, teachers in high-track classes were perceived by their students to present clearer instruction and to be more enthused about teaching. Even the social relationships and interactions among students were different. Oakes had confirmed, using a large data set, what researchers before her had suspected—that schools were reproducing the stratifications that existed in the culture at large.

A study conducted around the same time as Oakes's looked at the effect of tracking on teachers. Researcher Merrilee Finley found that teacher attitudes in the English department of the high school in which she taught reflected the hierarchical structure of the course offerings. Over time, teacher confidence and self-esteem became connected to their "track placement." Finley also found that the skills of teachers assigned to low-track classes appeared to diminish over time, providing low-track students with lesser-quality instruction.[7]

It is reasonable to wonder why the culture of low-tracked classrooms is so very different from that of the high-track class. In my interview with Jeannie Oakes, she spoke of the hours that she spent trying to create lessons that would intrigue and motivate her Basic English students. Try as she might, though, she always felt as though she was swimming against a powerful tide. She concluded that in low-track classes, students resist what the school has to teach as a way to challenge the school's control over their lives and their learning.

The literature on peer effects provides insight into how the student makeup of the classroom affects both achievement and culture. Looking at some 130 junior high school classes in mathematics and English, researchers Donald Veldman and Julie Sanford explored the complex relationship between "ability level" and achievement and behavior.[8] Veldman and Sanford used California Achievement Test scores to determine student ability, and a carefully constructed measure of outcomes was used to determine learning gains at the end of the year. Classroom observations were used to measure student and teacher behaviors in the studied classrooms.

The authors found that the achievement level of students in the class affected individual student performance. Not surprisingly, there was a strong relationship between the initial mean achievement level of the class and end-of-year assessment—the correlation was nearly perfect ($r = .93$ and $.95$). Individual pupil performance was predictable as well—higher achievers scored higher than lower achievers on the end-of-year test. What was most interesting, however, was that *both higher and lower achievers did better in the classes with a higher mean score, and that for lower achievers, this effect was greater than it was for higher achievers.* The significant effect on student achievement of classroom interaction with high achievers was found in both English and math classes. This finding provided evidence for Karl Alexander and Edward McDill's assertion that assignment to a high-track class advantaged students because of their exposure to high-track peers.[9]

Through meticulous observations, Veldman and Sanford determined that so-called lower-ability students were particularly more susceptible to peer effects in that they were more apt to act like the majority of students in the class. When lower-ability students were grouped together, they were more likely to be off-task and to adopt teacher-dependent behaviors. When there were higher achievers in the class, however, lower achievers were more likely to adopt the work habits and independent behaviors of their more school-proficient peers.

Whereas lower-ability students were more likely to act in a manner consistent with the class as a whole, higher-ability students were less dependent on class norms. The researchers speculated that beneficial peer modeling, in which lower-ability students emulate the good work behavior of the higher-ability majority in higher-ability classes, was the reason for the observed effect. In other words, one might expect lower-achieving students to work harder if they were placed in a higher-track or mixed-ability class.

Another plausible explanation is that teachers' expectations for behavior of lower-ability students may differ in higher- and lower-ability classes. Because it is a low-track class, over time the teacher may alter what she expects as good behavior and work habits. In low-track classes, teachers and students tend to engage in a feedback loop—students demonstrating a resistance to the norms of schooling, resulting in the teacher focusing on behavioral goals to create a classroom where learning can take place. This attempt by the teacher to control behavior often results in worksheet instruction designed to minimize student interactions, which in turn further bores and alienates students.

It comes as no surprise, then, that a 1968 National Education Association survey of teachers reported that less than 5 percent of all elementary school teachers, and less than 2 percent of all secondary school teachers, preferred to teach low-track classes.[10] Thirty-one years later, the National Research Council (NRC) would conclude, based on the preponderance of research showing overwhelmingly negative outcomes for students in low-track classes, that such classes, as presently designed, should not be utilized in educating students.[11] The NRC came to this conclusion having found no models of effective low-track classes in public schools.

RACIAL VARIANCES IN TRACK PLACEMENT

For Oakes, the most profound finding of her research was the racial stratification imposed by tracking. The integrated schools that the research team studied had pronounced racial patterns associated with tracked classes. Minority students were overrepresented in low-track classes and underrepresented in high-track classes. For white students, however, the reverse was true. Even vocational classes were tracked, with minority students taking low-level courses designed to prepare students for low-level occupations, such as dry cleaning and cosmetology. These courses were found predominantly in majority-minority schools and schools of mixed race. White students were more likely to be placed in vocational programs that focused on business and management. Very often, the programs designed to prepare students for low-level occupations were administered at off-campus locations. The business courses, in contrast, were taught on campus and were an integral part of the school day.[12]

As noted in chapter 1, the racial stratification caused by tracking was not lost on the courts or on the US Commission on Civil Rights. As researchers began to document the inequitable effects of tracking on students, parents—especially minority parents—sought relief through the justice system. Lawyers argued that tracking violated the equal protection clause of the Fourteenth Amendment. This is, of course, the same amendment that was used to strike down state "separate but equal" segregation laws in *Brown v. Board of Education*. Because public schools are part of the government, what they do is considered to be governmental action. In the Washington, DC, tracking case, *Hobson v. Hansen*, discussed in the previous chapter, Judge Skelly Wright based his finding that the DC schools' tracking system was discriminatory on the Fourteenth Amendment. He found the system itself to be "undemocratic and discriminatory" because the superintendent who created it did so to prepare some students for white-collar jobs and others for blue-collar employment, while not providing students a pathway to move from low track to high track.[13] However, on appeal (*Smuck v. Hobson*), the district was allowed to track as long as it remedied those mechanisms found to be discriminatory by Judge Wright.[14] In this case, tracking was allowed as long as track placement was not made on the basis of IQ test scores.

Most of the cases involving racial discrimination and tracking involved the resegregation of classrooms following court-ordered desegregation rulings. Even if such resegregation was not the deliberate aim of tracking, as appeared to be the case in *Hobson v. Hansen*, plaintiffs argued that it thwarted learning gains that might have resulted from desegregation.[15] Early cases that argued the segregation of classrooms as a result of tracking include *Moses v. Washington Parish School Board* (1971) and *McNeal v. Tate County School District* (1975). These cases established that while tracking is not in and of itself unconstitutional, if racially identifiable classes result, dual school districts (those with a history of prior segregation based on race) must demonstrate that tracking is not an extension of past segregation.[16] These decisions narrowed the scope of *Hobson v. Hansen*, in which the system itself was determined to be discriminatory, yet found a role for the courts in examining the discriminatory effects of tracking.

As mentioned in chapter 1, in 1976 the US Commission on Civil Rights issued a report regarding the progress made in court-ordered desegregated schools. That report noted that "the most common cause of classroom segregation was the educational practice of ability grouping."[17] The discriminatory effects of tracking were not exclusive to black students. The commission found, for example, that in the Southwest, Mexican American students were overrepresented in low-track classes and underrepresented in high-track ones. As the proportion of Mexican Americans in a school increased, so did their overrepresentation in the low track. In schools in which the Mexican American population exceeded 50 percent, more than three-quarters of the students in the low track were Mexican American.

The report also noted that the research on low-ability groups nearly always showed an unfavorable effect in regard to academic achievement, that the content of low-track courses was not demanding, and that teachers of these classes held low academic expectations for their students. The commission described low-track classes as dead end, their students as "trapped." It asserted that tracking systems "foreclose a student's chance for ever excelling."[18] The commission also noted that the courts had forbidden the use of IQ tests for assignment of minority students to educable mentally retarded (EMR) classes.

One of the districts included in the above study was the Stamford Public School System in Connecticut, the focus of a subsequent report issued in 1977.[19] This report provides rich insights into how a community debated its schools' tracking practices and the racial stratification that resulted. The commission acknowledged that it extensively discussed the issue of ability grouping in public hearings "because of its tendency to resegregate the classrooms with the middle- and high-income white students in the higher groups and the low-income black and Hispanic students in the lower groups."[20]

Although Stamford had detracked its elementary schools by 1972, there were four track levels in the middle schools. The report noted that the upper tracks were predominantly white and the lower tracks were predominantly African American.[21] The commission also noted that similar patterns existed in the high school: there was de facto segregation in both required classes and in electives.[22]

The Stamford report included interesting testimony from parents, teachers, and students, some of which was included in the national report. Some parents were in support of tracking, arguing that detracking would result in "white flight," while other parents argued for reforming the system. One black parent stated, "What the devil difference does it make if there is a kid in the class with a higher IQ than the other. . . . There are other factors of learning—how to live with people, how to live in this society, which are just so important."[23]

Students differed in their opinions as well. A white student argued that tracking was preferable because "students learn at different rates." Black and Latino students disagreed. In describing the culture of the low-track classes, one black student remarked that the grouping system "makes them [blacks] feel like they are lower."[24] Students also reported that teachers had lower expectations of students in the lower tracks, and several Latino and black students believed that the better teachers were assigned to the top groups and that teachers in the lower group were less interested in their students and were there primarily to control student behavior.

From the research, as well as from data collected from civil rights studies and court cases, a clear pattern was emerging: there was a distinct difference between the instruction, performance, attitudes, expectations, and racial composition of low-track versus high-track classes. Tracking was quickly being seen as creating a restricted learning environment for minority students, and some researchers argued that it very well might be a contributor to the nation's racial achievement gap in learning outcomes.[25]

Researchers then focused on measuring the extent of stratification by race and socioeconomic status caused by tracking and the reasons why such stratification was occurring. After the publication of *Keeping Track*, Jeannie Oakes went to the RAND Institute for Civil Justice as a policy analyst, where she would continue her work analyzing the effects of tracking. In 1985, Rand received a grant from the National Science Foundation to investigate the racial achievement gap in the study of advanced math and science. Oakes was perfectly positioned to do that work. Tracking was on the front burner as a school practice that was contributing to the learning outcome gap among the nation's races.

3
Tracking and Classroom Segregation

Judge Skelly Wright understood tracking for what it was—a means by which to continue segregation within Washington, DC, schools that had been forced to desegregate. He understood the basic inequities inherent in tracking systems. Those who later ruled on his decision, however, had a different perspective. They did not question the need for a tracking system. They assumed that if a means other than IQ testing was used, the track-placement process could be fixed, tracking would be fair, and school tracks would not be stratified by race and class.

Nearly everyone, however, did acknowledge that there was a problem. Students of color and students of poverty continued to be noticeably absent from advanced courses in mathematics and science. What was it about tracking and track placement that was causing such inequities to exist? Was the nature of tracking itself to blame, or were misguided track-placement policies at fault?

EXAMINING INEQUITIES IN TRACK PLACEMENT

After the publication of *Keeping Track*, the topic of tracking moved front and center as an area of education research. During the 1980s and 1990s, national databases became rich sources of information through a process known as best-evidence synthesis. The findings of individual studies, along with research derived from new studies, was utilized in order to determine the general effects of tracking on student achievement and classroom demographics.[1] Once again, Jeannie Oakes was at the forefront.

While at the RAND Institute, Oakes, along with colleagues Tor Ormseth, Robert Bell, and Patricia Camp, engaged in a major research project to determine the rates of participation in science and math classes of minority students, students of low socioeconomic status (SES), and women.[2] Not surprisingly, they identified tracking as a prime contributor to the opportunity gap in math and science. Their findings included the following:

In integrated schools, classes in which there were large numbers of minority students were more often perceived by teachers and students to be "low ability" classes.

Less-challenging math and science courses had larger percentages of low-SES and minority students in attendance.

In schools in which low-SES students comprised the vast majority of students, there were fewer challenging math and science courses, especially "gatekeeper" courses such as accelerated algebra.[3] Even the college-prep track at such schools had fewer academic courses.

Teachers of low-track classes in every school included in the study were less experienced and had fewer credentials, even when controlling for school type.

It was apparent in the 1980s and 1990s that the patterns of stratification that had resulted in litigation after court-ordered desegregation persisted. Even though schools were more cognizant of how tracking practices resulted in segregated classrooms, little had been done to address the problem. Research studies continued to demonstrate that in integrated schools, black and Latino students were dramatically overrepresented in low-track classes and underrepresented in high-track classes.[4] Race was not the only factor associated with track placement, however. Researchers found that socioeconomic status played a role as well.[5] One study found that a highly proficient student (that is, a student with top test scores) from a low-SES background had slightly better than a 50 percent chance of being placed in a high-track class.[6] Because ethnic and racial factors are associated with low economic status, black and Latino students were at a disproportionate disadvantage.[7]

Why such patterns existed became an important research question. Was the observed stratification a result of differences in the intellectual promise and achievement of students, or was it a result of prejudice and low expectations? What role did poverty play? How did parental advocacy affect track placement?

The commonly held belief was, and still is, that variance in academic performance is the primary reason for class and racial differences in school-tracking placements. That was certainly the position of tracking proponents, who claimed that the system was both race-neutral and fair. Researchers were not so sure.

To test whether academic performance played the main role in track placement, prior achievement, usually measured by standardized test scores, was included as a control in regression models in order to determine whether stratification by race and class was the result of objective measures of students' learning. In other words, if track placement was neutral in regard to race and class, then one would expect that students with the same prior achievement would be placed in the same track. Regression analysis allows researchers to answer such questions because it holds achievement steady as a variable in examining outcomes.

When all the data was analyzed, however, track placements were found to be less than fair. Researchers determined that although prior achievement could explain *some* of the race and class stratification found in tracked systems, it was an incomplete explanation. When studies controlled for prior academic performance, students from high-SES homes were (and still are) overrepresented in the academic track, and students from low-SES homes were underrepresented in the high track.[8]

The idea that something other than an objective measure of achievement was the reason for racial stratification in tracking systems was rejected outright by some researchers. Defenders of tracking argued that racial stratification is an artifact of achievement differences and that, when achievement is controlled for, black students have a placement advantage in high-track classes.[9] This position implies that black students are placed in high tracks via unspoken affirmative action policies—a claim that is not supported by research that looked at that very question.[10]

CONTINUING INVOLVEMENT OF THE COURTS

Tracking was consistently being associated with inequitable opportunity, and Jeannie Oakes's work was being widely disseminated and discussed by researchers, teachers, and school administrators alike. After four years at RAND, Oakes returned to UCLA, where she continued her research, serving as a mentor to others who were interested in questions of equity and tracking. One of her star pupils was a young lawyer, Kevin Welner.[11]

In the late 1970s, when Welner was a student in his local California high school, he'd never questioned the tracking system. Because the system was rigid, and he had transferred into the district too late to be tested for the "gifted" track, he was placed in the second-highest track. In this regard he may have been a victim of tracking, but because the upper-middle-class students in his "college prep" classes were serious and focused on their studies, there was little reason for complaint. It was a good environment in which to learn.

It was not until he was a high school senior that he began to think about tracking. His English teacher, Marlyn Whirry, who would later become the 2000 National Teacher of the Year, talked privately with him and some other students about the school's tracking system. She saw tracking as a barrier to learning. She pointed out that while she taught all levels of English, she utilized the same curriculum and employed the same demanding style across tracks—and she found that all her students could meet the challenge. She saw tracking's inequities, and she was not shy about sharing her thoughts and insights with her students. Kevin Welner took notice.

After obtaining a law degree from UCLA, Welner spent four years practicing law in Los Angeles before deciding to enter the world of education policy. He returned to UCLA, and during his second year in the doctoral program he began working with Jeannie Oakes. When Oakes was hired to serve as an expert witness on litigation that challenged tracking as a form of second-generation segregation, Welner, with his background in the law, was well positioned to assist her. Through his legal and course work he'd developed a deep understanding of the issues around tracking, achievement, and race.

Oakes and Welner immersed themselves in cases in four districts, studying tracking policies and detracking efforts: Rockford, Illinois; San Jose, California; Wilmington, Delaware; and Woodland Hills, Pennsylvania. They participated in the actual litigation in all but Woodland Hills, which by the time they got involved was already under a court order to detrack.

The four systems had been ordered by the courts to detrack in order to obtain unitary status.[12] By way of background, following the *Brown* decision, districts that were found to be operating separate (or "dual") systems for black and white students were ordered by the courts to desegregate. After doing so, districts returned to the courts asking them to find that they had remedied that violation and had reached "unitary status." In some cases, this request was denied if it was determined that other systems, such as tracking, created de facto segregation.

For instance, the Woodland Hills School District in Pennsylvania was ordered by the court to desegregate in 1981 and to detrack in 1988, due to the court's findings that the district's identification process for grouping special education and gifted education resulted in classrooms that were identifiable by race. Similarly, in 1994, the court ordered that the schools of San Jose, California, detrack in a graduated way (some tracking allowed at the secondary level, but complete detracking at the elementary level) as a modification to its original school desegregation order.

That same year, the court found that the Rockford, Illinois, school district engaged in "intentional system wide discrimination against African American and Latino students" and proposed detracking as a necessary remedy.[13] A three-judge appellate panel later overturned the mandated detracking, considering it to be too restrictive. The final case they studied concerned the school districts in Wilmington, Delaware. In 1978, the courts had found that the state and the districts had changed district boundary lines to purposefully segregate schools. Three years later, the court found that while the schools themselves were desegregated, tracking and ability grouping had resegregated classrooms.

In each of the four districts, Welner and Oakes studied the data, interviewed teachers and parents, discussed detracking strategies (and obstacles) with school leaders, and attended public meetings.

In his book *Legal Rights, Local Wrongs*, Welner presents a detailed description of the process and politics encountered by the districts. He also describes the racial disparity in track placement that resulted in the court orders to detrack. In the districts, African American or Latino students of comparable achievement to white students (as measured by standardized test scores) were far more likely to be placed in lower math and English tracks, and far less likely to be placed in higher math or English tracks. Some of the data that describes that discrepancy follows.

In the San Jose public schools, white and Asian American students with average scores on standardized tests were more than twice as likely to be in "accelerated" classes as Latinos with the same scores. The gap that results from differing placement along the lines of ethnicity are even wider in some bands of achievement for ninth-grade college-prep classes, as illustrated in table 3.1.

Welner reported several key findings. First, the tracked classes were not truly academically homogeneous groups. Although the intent of tracking is to create such homogeneity for instructional purposes, the classes that he and Oakes studied—however they were outwardly labeled—included a wide range of students in terms of standardized test scores. Second, as noted above, the districts tended to enroll Latino and African American students disproportionately in lower-tracked classes, and this pattern shows up even once the researchers controlled for prior measured achievement. Third, once students began on the "low track," they did not move to a higher track, and their academic performance continued to deteriorate. The achievement

Table 3.1
Likelihood of Placement in San Jose College-Prep
Math Course (Grade 9) (1985–1992)

ACHIEVEMENT SCORE	LATINO	WHITE	ASIAN AMERICAN
40–49	1.8%	11.1%	26.7%
50–59	9.3%	24.2%	68.7%
60–69	24.1%	56.5%	57.7%
70–79	50.0%	64.4%	88.0%
80–89	—	80.9%	86.7%
90–99	56.3%	93.3%	97.3%

Does not include data if fewer than fifteen students.

Source: Kevin G. Welner, *Legal Rights, Local Wrongs: When Community Control Collides with Educational Equity* (Albany: State University of New York, 2001), 62.

data showed that students who began at the same achievement level, but were in the low-track classes, experienced less growth than those in the average or high track. If the purpose of low-track classes was to remediate their learning, they were a dismal failure.

The research done by Oakes and Welner in the four districts became important courtroom testimony. It also became a source of guidance for the detracking districts as they navigated difficult reform in systems rife with conflict and racial tension. Chapter 7 tells the story of one of those districts, Woodland Hills, as it sought to provide more equitable learning opportunities to its students while working toward achieving unitary status.

RESEARCH ON CAUSES OF TRACK STRATIFICATION

Oakes, Welner, and other researchers clearly identified the degree of racial stratification among tracks, but an even more complex question remained—what *caused* the inequitable placements in the first place? Although the observed stratification may have been partly a result of prior achievement combined with race and class prejudice, other factors were also shown to be at play in influencing track assignment. The work of Elizabeth Useem gives us insight into the role parents play in student track placement.

Useem looked at accelerated-math-class placement in middle schools. Accelerated math is the highest math track in middle school, participation in which puts students on a pathway to the study of calculus in grade twelve. When listed on the high school transcript, calculus is a signal to college admissions officers that the student is of "high ability."[14]

Useem's study of twenty-six school districts in the Greater Boston area found that placement criteria varied widely from district to district.[15] She also found that parents with college and advanced degrees are more likely to intervene in school experiences, resulting in their child's placement in accelerated math classes. In a study of two geographically adjacent and demographically similar middle schools in the Boston area, Useem found that there were important differences in two areas: parental knowledge of their child's math-class placement, and the degree of influence they exerted on that placement. Highly educated parents were more "in the know," and were not afraid to use their knowledge and social capital to get their children into the high-track math class.

This phenomenon of middle-class parents "working the system" to gain advantage for their child has been documented at the elementary level as well.[16] On the other hand, Useem found that parents with fewer years of schooling were more inclined to trust the decision of the educators in regard to their child's math placement and that their primary focus was on their child's grades rather than the difficulty level of the course.

Schools were faced with a conundrum. They realized there was something inherently wrong with a system that would create such stratification, but it appeared to be very difficult to come up with policies that would result in racial and socioeconomic balance in classrooms. In an attempt to overcome all the complex factors that lead to racially and socioeconomically stratified classes, some schools began to allow parents and students to choose their track. Some schools required students to maintain a minimum grade to stay in a high-track class, while others left the decision entirely to the family.

In a 2002 study, Susan Yonezawa, Amy Stuart Wells, and Irene Serna studied ten racially diverse schools that allowed students to choose their track as a way to provide more challenging opportunities for all students and to integrate the school's classrooms.[17] What they found was both surprising and disappointing.

Even when students were allowed to choose their track, the same patterns of stratification occurred. Few black and Latino students from low- and middle-track classes opted to move into high-track classes in these racially mixed schools. The reasons were complex and many.

First, it appeared that the information regarding track choice was not evenly communicated among student groups. There was no attempt at outreach to spread the word about the importance of taking high-track classes. Although middle- and upper-class parents well understood the choice system, poor parents did not. In addition, minority students complained to the researchers that their desire to enroll in a higher track was not taken seriously by their school counselors.

As the researchers conducted their interviews they also found that some counselors and teachers created barriers by telling students that they needed prerequisite courses, or, in one case, by giving students a reading test. Students also reported getting mixed messages from school personnel regarding their ability to do the work. In contrast, more affluent white students well understood the importance of high-track classes, were encouraged by staff to enroll in them, and used the choice system to gain educational advantage.

Finally, they found that black students were susceptible to peer pressure that led them to lower-track classes. These students expressed the concern that if they chose the high-track class, they would be the only black students in the class, and thus ostracized by their friends who remained in the lower tracks. They reported feeling supported by peers in the lower-track classes, but pressured to prove their worthiness in high-track classes—both to the other students and to the teacher.

According to the authors, the complex interactions between class, race, tracks, and aspirations persisted, even when the barriers for movement to higher tracks were dismantled. In summary, Yonezawa, Wells, and Serna found that even in systems of choice, institutional barriers remain, and many minority students would not leave low- and middle-track classes for social reasons, peer pressure, and lack of confidence.

The authors concluded that although choice may be well intentioned, the structure of tracking resulted in the same stratification. Their recommendation was that the tracking system itself be dismantled."[18]

Researchers may never be able to identify all the complex factors, and their interactions, that result in the stratification associated with tracking. For the present, it is important for the reader to know that despite decades of trying to eliminate racial stratification associated with tracking, inequities persist. Whether it is placement by parental and student choice, placement by counselors, or placement by test scores, the same patterns of inequality result.

STRATIFICATION ACROSS SCHOOLS

The same kind of stratification found in tracking systems within schools also occurs across school systems that combine choice with entrance criteria. Several years ago, I addressed a group of outstanding New York City principals who attended a summer academy at Teachers College, Columbia University. Although they agreed with my perspective that eliminating tracking and giving all students the same high-level curriculum improves achievement, they were puzzled as to how their students could receive the benefits of such reform. They were frustrated that high achievers had been pulled out of their schools, and dismayed by the lack of racial and socioeconomic diversity within their student bodies. It was as if the choice system, especially at the middle and high school levels, requiring students to go through both an application and a screening process, had transformed the New York City schools into one vast tracking system. School choice was resulting in the same problems that Yonezawa and her team found with track choice.

The "tracking writ large" caused by school choice policies was so problematic that in 2013 a formal complaint was filed on behalf of individual parents as well as local civil rights groups to the Office of Civil Rights of the US Department of Education. The complaint alleged that the policy had a disparate negative impact on African American and Latino students because, due to the sorting policies of choice such as screening, they were more likely to attend schools that included high concentrations of students who were "high needs"—defined by the plaintiffs as students who were overage for their class and substantially behind in credits.[19] The details of the complaint, as well as the studies that led to its filing, will be discussed in the final chapter.

Racial balance is difficult to achieve in New York City. The public schools serve a predominantly black and Latino student body (77 percent), with the rest of the school population being about evenly divided between white and Asian American students. However, choice/test-in policies exacerbate stratification, as table 3.2 illustrates.[20]

The first three schools are unscreened high schools. At all three, when compared with the overall diversity of New York City schools, minority students and students who receive free and reduced-priced lunch are clearly overrepresented. With more than 95 percent of their student bodies being either black or Latino, they are examples of extreme racial isolation.

Table 3.2
Demographics of Selected NYC High Schools: 2010 Report

OPEN-ENROLLMENT SCHOOLS	ASIAN	BLACK	LATINO	WHITE	FRPL
Far Rockaway	3%	52%	44%	1%	96%
Maxwell Career and Technical High School	1%	72%	24%	1%	84%
Paul Robeson High School	1%	89%	9%	1%	78%
TEST-IN OR SCREENED					
Stuyvesant	67%	2%	3%	26%	13%
Bronx High School of Science	64%	3%	8%	25%	24%
Eleanor Roosevelt	20%	7%	10%	63%	19%
NYC Overall	15%	30%	40%	15%	67%

The "test-in" schools, such as Stuyvesant High School and the Bronx High School of Science, known as specialized high schools, are among the city's eight most prestigious. They are disproportionally white and Asian. Entrance into these schools is based solely on performance on one test, the Specialized High Schools Admissions Test.[21] Clearly, despite court decisions of the past century that cautioned schools not to track students using test scores, tests are being used to sort students into competitive high schools.

The lack of diversity in test-in schools has been well known to the New York City Department of Education, but nothing has changed to ameliorate the inequities.[22] In a 2008 critique of the admissions test, Joshua Feinman discussed the racial disparities in admissions that it produces.[23] He also questioned whether one test should be the sole gatekeeper of admissions, noting that some students have access to test prep for the test while others do not. Feinman contrasted the test-based admissions policy with the multiple-criteria policy used by Thomas Jefferson Science and Technology High School in Virginia. Despite the additional criteria, however, black and Latino students comprise less than 5 percent of that school's enrollment.[24]

The wide disparities in enrollment have not gone unnoticed by those concerned with civil rights and equal opportunity. In addition to the 2013 complaint to the Office of Civil Rights mentioned above, the NAACP recently filed a complaint regarding the New York City test-in schools based on what it believes is a flawed test. The test is seen as discriminatory against black and Latino students and a breach of the Civil Rights Act on the basis of its "unjustified, racially disparate impact."[25]

There are other selection models in addition to "test-in." Eleanor Roosevelt High School is a small school on the Upper East Side of Manhattan. It is a screened school program that chooses students based on grades, standardized test scores, and attendance information, but does only a slightly better job of attracting a diverse student body. Despite the wider entrance criteria, only 17 percent of its students are Latino or black, far fewer than the proportional 70 percent of black and Latino students in the city's schools. Sixty-three percent of its student body is white even though the overall proportion in the city of white students is 15 percent.

Research on tiered schooling in other nations found that being in a "high ability" school is associated with higher achievement and that tiered international systems that couple tracking with curriculum differentiation lead to high levels of inequality and exacerbate the achievement gap. One recent study indicated that tiered schooling might be responsible for decreases (or increases) in student IQ scores. A team of German psychologists examined the effects of vocational-school enrollment on the development of student intelligence. That study found that students in academic tracks experienced substantial intelligence (IQ) gains as compared to students in nonacademic, vocational tracks in state schools.[26]

We have long known that achievement accelerates in the academic track as compared with the vocational track; this study shows that intelligence itself grows at an accelerated rate in academic programs as opposed to vocational programs. And this phenomenon is not limited to this single study or to Germany. It was first observed in studies in Sweden in 1968, 1982, and 1991. In addition, two researchers in Israel in 1988 found similar findings regarding tracking's effect on the growth of intelligence between the academic and vocational track, even after controlling for prior testing and family background.

The relationship between race, SES, and student sorting practices, whether they exist at the building or district level, play out in predictable ways, regardless of the method used to sort. As Jeannie Oakes noted, they are not equity-neutral. That is why it is critical that we examine their effectiveness as a mechanism for better educating students. If tracking is effective in raising student achievement, then perhaps there is a tradeoff that makes it worthwhile. If, however, grouping practices are ineffective in raising achievement, or if they create winners and losers, than their continuance cannot be justified. Chapter 4 examines that very question.

4

Tracking and Student Achievement

After researchers exposed the racial and socioeconomic stratification associated with tracking, and unequal access to high-track classes, they were confronted with answering the most important question of all: Knowing what we know about tracking's inequities, should we advise that it be abolished? Racial and class stratification was a clear result of tracking, whether segregation was the intent or not. There were no truly "objective" systems of track placement—schools had different systems and parental pressure certainly played a role. There was only one argument, then, that could support its continuance—tracking could only be justified if it could be clearly demonstrated that it was associated with higher student achievement. In other words, if it could be shown that students learned more because of tracking, and that low-track classes actually remediated learning, then perhaps all the other problems associated with tracking were worth bearing.

Studying the achievement effects of an educational intervention is not easy. Truth be told, educational research is a messy business.

This is because there are so many factors that we know influence student learning. There are class size effects, resource effects, teacher effects (experience, certification status, and skill), curricular effects, and leadership effects. Background characteristics certainly affect achievement—race, ethnicity, parents' education, socioeconomic status—all play a role and must be accounted for in measurement models. We know that peer effects (the influence that fellow class or schoolmates have on whole-class or whole-school learning) matter. Attendance rates matter as well as student retention rates. Some of the above matter a lot, others seem to matter less. In addition, often several of the above will interact, producing a new set of effects as well.

The above variables demonstrate just how difficult it is to measure the effect of any contribution to achievement outcomes. After all is said and done, and all of the relevant contributors are added and subtracted from the statistical model, there is still variation that cannot be described. Researchers often refer to it as "noise"—those factors yet to be identified which nevertheless contribute to achievement.

It is no wonder, then, that when a practice as controversial as tracking became the subject of studies on student achievement, there were claims, counterclaims, battles over methodology, and value judgments based on varying interpretations of findings. There is, on the surface, a superficial logic to tracking that appeals to the public and to parents. No one wants students to be left behind, or to have the learning of some students slowed down. Before I became a teacher, and experienced tracked classes from an instructional point of view, I myself never challenged the practice. In the beginning, like Jeannie Oakes, I kept trying to make my low-track classes "work," until I came to the realization that it was the system, not the students or the teacher, that was the problem. Below I've presented some of the research showing why this is so.

MEASURING THE EFFECTS OF TRACKING

Researchers looked at the achievement effects of tracking in one of two ways. The first way was to compare students who were tracked to students who were not tracked (track/no track studies). These studies are of two methodological types: experimental and quasi-experimental. In the first instance, students were randomly assigned, or matched-pair assigned, to either tracked or untracked classrooms. The other type used an approach in which the performance of matched groups of students in schools or classrooms that track, or do not track, was then compared with each other.

The second way that researchers looked at the effects of tracking was the use of high-track/low-track studies in which researchers attempted to compare the achievement of students in high-track classes with the achievement of students in low-track classes. Because these are nonexperimental studies, researchers controlled as best they could for the effects of the factors described in the beginning of this chapter, such as prior achievement and socioeconomic status. The purpose of these studies was to measure the effects of different track placements.

Track/No Track Studies

Several decades ago, researcher Robert Slavin analyzed numerous experimental studies of tracking to determine whether or not tracking was an effective way to improve student learning.[1] Slavin's best-evidence synthesis of secondary-level tracking included studies that used standardized or teacher-created tests to measure student achievement, and used random or matched assignment of students to grouped or ungrouped classes based on achievement. He concluded that tracking's effect on student achievement was "indistinguishable from zero," not only for all groups combined, but for each track level as well.[2]

In other words, Slavin found that grouping students for instruction based on previous achievement has no effect on learning when all groups are taught the same curriculum. Slavin argued that such studies are the only accurate assessment of tracking, because they exclusively measure the effects of grouping, not curriculum differentiation. He also argued that if tracking has no achievement effects, and it results in racial-class stratification, then we should not track at all.

Two other researchers, James Kulik and Chien-Lin Kulik, found results similar to Slavin's in their 1982 meta-analysis.[3] While the Kulik study found no overall significant difference in tracked and untracked classes for "lower and middle ability students," it did find a very slight increase in learning (.1 year gain in growth) for the "higher aptitude student" in grouped classes. The differences between the two meta-analyses are attributable to the studies included by the researchers.

Recently, Ning Rui from the University of Pennsylvania took on the challenge of conducting a new review of studies using the four decades of research that is now available.[4] Rui conducted a meta-analysis of fifteen studies that examined tracked versus nontracked educational settings between 1972 and 2006. His findings on achievement effects were clear—detracking benefited low achievers without hurting the achievement of average and high achievers. There was no advantage to tracking for anyone, and clear advantages to detracking for lower-track students.

High-Track/Low-Track Studies

High-track/low-track studies seek to measure the effects of track placement on a variety of student outcomes, especially the measurement of student achievement. In such studies, students in high-track classes are compared with students in low-track classes.

One of the first studies took place in 1982. Karl Alexander and Martha Cook compared the effects of high-track/low-track placement using data from eight high schools included in a 1961–69 study by the Educational Testing Service.[5] After controlling for a variety of factors, including previous achievement, they found that track placement had no significant effect on student achievement. The majority of studies, however, did find that tracking made a difference—high-track classes gave advantage to the students in the class, while low-track classes had negative effects on the students in those classes. Using national data from the 1980 High School and Beyond Survey, Adam Gamoran and Robert Mare found that being in the college-prep track improved student achievement in the senior year; the net advantage to students of being in the college math track as opposed to the non-college-bound math track was nearly 21 percent.[6] Some of the early studies showed that the "high-track advantage" over the bottom track was enormous—one found that the achievement gap between high-track students and low-track students exceeded the gap between students who remained in school and those who dropped out.[7]

While additional studies continued to confirm the advantage of being in a high-track and the disadvantage of being in a low-track class, it was also becoming clear that gains experienced by high achievers were being accrued at the expense of low achievers.[8]

The pattern of low-track student disadvantage continued to appear in study after study, beyond the borders of the United States. Alan Kerckhoff replicated high-track/low-track effects in British schools.[9] He found that high-track students were advantaged while low-track students fell behind. The group most adversely affected was students in remedial groups. Kerckhoff describes students in remedial reading classes as experiencing no remediation of their skills at all.

THE TRACKING WARS

The track/no track studies demonstrated that one group of students might be benefitting from tracking at another's expense. What was not clear was whether detracking would solve the problem without hurting some students—that is, would high achievers lose if schools detracked? In the 1990s, the results of Rui's meta-analysis were not available, and there were few studies other than the early studies of Slavin and Kulik.

And so a group of researchers tried to use a national database to answer that question. Dominic Brewer and his colleagues used data from the National Educational Longitudinal Study of 1988 (NELS:88) to study the effect of tenth-grade mathematics tracking on student achievement, comparing tracked to nontracked classes.[10] These researchers found that tracking caused decreased achievement for low-track students and increased achievement for students in the high track. The authors went one step further and attempted to estimate the effect of detracking on learning. They estimated that detracking would result in an 8.7 percent gain in math scores on an Educational Testing Service–developed test of cognitive skills for students in low-track classes and an 8.1 percent decrease in scores of students in high-track classes. The researchers estimated a 1.7 percent decline in the scores of students in classrooms described as containing students of average achievement.

According to these authors, if detracking occurred, high-performing students would experience substantial reduced achievement, and low-track students would experience great gains. The authors acknowledged, however, that it was impossible to disentangle the effects of different curricula from the effects of tracking. There were also not many examples of detracked tenth-grade math classes for comparison, and what was designated an advanced class in one district might not be considered advanced in another. That study would later be one of the fifteen studies included in Rui's 2009 meta-analysis. As noted earlier, in the meta-analysis, the conclusion of Brewer and his co-researchers was not typical.

In the final decade of the twentieth century, however, this study became a rallying point for those who supported tracking. The argument was framed in terms of winners and losers. The winners were the high-track students, while the losers were those students relegated to low-track classes. Those who supported tracking had no problem putting the needs of high achievers first.

Stiff resistance came from advocates of gifted education, and that resistance emphasized the "high track advantage." In a 1999 book, *The Tracking Wars*, one of the most outspoken researchers on the topic, Tom Loveless, chronicled the tensions surrounding detracking efforts in California and Massachusetts.[11] Loveless, a former teacher of the gifted, argued that detracking hurts high achievers, and speculated that it would result in "bright flight." Although there was no evidence of effective low-track classes in public schools, he, and other supporters of tracking, insisted that reform, not abandonment, was the solution.

The problem was, no one knew how to reform low-track classes. When I was an assistant principal, I thought surely there was a way. I had a small group of special education and low-achieving students whom I placed together in a math class because I believed it would give them the support they needed. The class was a double-period class with a general education teacher, a special education teacher, and a teaching assistant. I also brought in a top-notch staff developer to work with the class. No matter what I did, however, the class was problematic. Students were off-task and often disruptive. Their academic progress was slow. Worst of all, the class kept growing in size as counselors saw it as the solution for struggling students and an appropriate placement for new entrants to the school who had never taken algebra.

In an attempt to "save" the class, I began transferring the most disruptive students into the higher-track class. Each time this happened, the achievement of the relocated student improved and another student stepped up to lead the disruption in the low-track class. Like Jeannie Oakes discovered so many years before, low-track classes do a disservice to the students in them and the teachers who teach them. Rarely do you ever find a parent who says, "Please put my child in the low-track class."

When we look at the results of high track/low track studies in the light of the anecdote that I just shared, we begin to understand the dynamics of tracking. High track/low track studies furthered our knowledge of the effects of tracking on achievement, and they certainly produced debate. However, there were limitations to what they could tell us. Although the studies attempted to control for factors that affect student performance, many of these factors either were not or could not be included.

In addition, the identification of track placement in large national studies such as NELS:88 rely on teacher or student reports. As noted in chapter 1, students frequently misperceive their track placement.[12] Likewise, researchers questioned whether questionnaires like NELS that ask teachers to describe the level of the students they teach, rather than to identify the track they teach, result in accurate identification of tracks.[13]

Finally, and perhaps most importantly, when a study determines that a high-track advantage exists, it is impossible to ascertain what actually causes the effect.

As discussed earlier, Oakes found that students in high-track classes receive higher-quality instruction. At least in the case of mathematics, high-track classes are more likely to be taught by teachers who received their degree in the subject. Low-track classes, in contrast, are more often taught by nonspecialist teachers whose skills diminish over time. It bears repeating that in 1999 the National Research Council concluded, based on the overwhelmingly negative research regarding low-track classes, that students should not be educated in low-track classes as they were designed.[14]

By the turn of the twenty-first century, there were few who argued that low-track classes were good learning environments for students. It was clear that these classes inhibited the learning potential of the students placed in them. The argument shifted, then, to the needs of advanced students, like the boy with the purple tie introduced in chapter 1. Advocates of tracking argued that meeting the needs of the gifted and talented was important for national well-being.

Educators were told to fix the low track but leave the high track alone. Those open to detracking schools wondered whether such reform would come at the expense of high achievers. It was time to take a deeper look at this question.

EXAMINING THE HIGH-TRACK ADVANTAGE

What was it, exactly, that accounted for the "high-track advantage"? Was it peer effects? Superior instruction? More effective curriculum? A combination of factors? Studies had shown a variety of contributors to student learning that were strongly associated with high tracks.

Could it be that if all students were given access to the high-track curriculum, all would benefit, even high achievers?

Some researchers responded yes. Jeannie Oakes and her colleagues argued that tracked classes should be replaced by heterogeneous classes teaching an enriched curriculum. Detracking should be a process of "leveling up" and providing support.

The defenders of tracking, including James Kulik and Tom Loveless, however, contended that differentiated curriculum is essential and that without it, high-achieving students would go unchallenged. Their solution to achievement inequities associated with tracking was to fix the low track—although they were unable to point to one example of excellent low-track instruction.

Studies of tracking that provided insight into whether or not detracked classes with high-track curriculum might be an effective solution indicated that Oakes was correct. Let's examine what happens when—either by accident or by design—traditionally low- or average-track students are leveled up and given the high-track curriculum.

RESEARCH ON ACCELERATED LEARNING

Accelerated classes began as an attempt to meet the needs of "gifted and talented" learners. The tradition began in the nineteenth century with programs such as the Cambridge Double Track Plan of 1891, and the special progress classes of the New York City Schools.[15] More recently, researchers have encouraged the use of accelerated curriculum for disadvantaged learners who are generally assigned to remedial classrooms.[16] Based on the poor results of traditional remedial and low-track programs, these researchers contend that the instruction of low-achieving students should be accelerated rather than slowed down, in order to increase student learning. The following three studies give insight into what occurs, with the learning of both the lower and higher achievers in the class, when you do just that. All three examples are from mathematics classes—the subject that the opponents of detracking claim is most difficult to detrack.

The first example describes what occurred in Missouri when average achievers were placed in a high-track class in math.[17]

Average Achievers in the High-Track Class

In this study, thirty-four seventh-grade students of average achievement were assigned to the advanced eighth-grade pre-algebra class. Ten of the thirty-four students scored below the fiftieth percentile on a norm-referenced achievement test, the Comprehensive Assessment Program Achievement Series Test (CAP). The teacher of the class was directed to employ active instruction and to maintain the high standards she held in previous years; in other words, she was not to lower her standards or to attempt to "teach to the middle." Both the high-achieving and average-achieving students who comprised the three sections of this experimental class were compared with high and average achievers from two previous cohorts.

The researchers found improved performance for the average achievers on both the standardized test, the CAP, and a two-hour comprehensive, teacher-developed test of pre-algebra skills. When the performance of the average-achieving accelerated students on the CAP was compared with the performance of similar students in the past two cohorts, a significant increase in achievement in the area of mathematical concepts was found.

The other two dimensions of math proficiency measured by the CAP were computation and problem solving. For average achievers, computation remained stable when compared with students in previous cohorts, and problem solving was up, although not by a statistically significant amount. In addition, the performance of the high-achieving students was maintained, as measured by the CAP; they did not achieve less due to the presence of students of average math achievement in their class, and on one measure—concepts —their performance demonstrated a significant increase when compared with the performance of the two previous cohorts. The presence of lower achievers in the class did not hurt the learning of higher achievers, and when it came to conceptual understanding, their achievement improved.

Average- and high-achieving student performance was also compared using the teacher-developed test to more fully measure pre-algebra skills. Considerable score overlap among the students was found, with some average achievers outperforming high achievers!

Based on their findings, the authors concluded that the school needed to change its tracking policy. According to their results, students of average or low-average proficiency were being denied access to courses without justification.

One of the most interesting findings of the study were the long-term effects on math achievement. The average-achieving students assigned to the high-track classes later enrolled in more high school advanced mathematics courses than did students of like achievement in previous cohorts—an average increase of 1.5 more advanced classes than the 1983–84 cohort and 1.0 more than the 1982–83 cohort. The authors believed that the difference would have been even greater if the high school had not "downtracked" half of the average achievers who had participated in the advanced class, even though they had achieved scores in the mastery range on the eighth-grade test.

Although this study was single school and small in scale, it provided insight for those who considered the idea of breaking the tracking mold and putting more students into high-track classes. It would later give support to those who would take a more courageous move, and give all students high-track curriculum in detracked class-rooms.

The Accelerated Schools Project

The second example is a large, formal study of accelerating the learning of students at risk of failure. An analysis of the Accelerated Schools Project, developed by Henry M. Levin, demonstrated that enriched, accelerated learning experiences for children at risk of school failure produce gains in both reading and mathematics.[18] Accelerated schools use a combination of challenging materials and high expectations, similar to strategies used in classes for the academically gifted. In accelerated schools, changes in curriculum and teaching occur within a whole-school reform model intended to transform school culture.

Manpower Demonstration Research Corporation did an independent evaluation of the model during the 1990s. MDRC studied eight elementary schools across the nation that adopted the Accelerated Schools Model during their first five years of implementation. Its report, which was issued in in 2001, demonstrated a significant gain of .24 standard deviations in the average third-grade mathematics score when compared with the three-year baseline mean score prior to acceleration. Scores that were below the national average moved above the national average, with the greatest improvements seen for students in the initial lowest-performing schools.

Low Achievers in the High-Track Class

The third example explored the effects of accelerating students of the lowest achievement into high-track classes. John M. Peterson, a professor of mathematics at Brigham Young University, conducted a research study in three demographically similar Utah school districts that compared the effects of differentiated junior high math programs on students identified as remedial, average, or accelerated.[19] Student identification was made based on scores achieved on the California Test of Basic Skills as well as IQ scores. Seventh-grade remedial students were divided into three groups and placed into either a remedial class, a class with average curriculum moving at a slower pace, or a heterogeneously grouped accelerated pre-algebra course.

The remedial students who were placed in the untracked and accelerated pre-algebra class showed significant improvement in math skills as compared with the remedial students in either the remedial program or the regular seventh-grade curriculum. The Peterson study provided evidence that students of the lowest achievement level benefit more from studying the accelerated curriculum designed for the most proficient students than from the remedial curriculum supposedly designed to meet the needs of low-achieving students.

Students Misplaced in Higher-Track Classes

As noted earlier in this book, track assignment is far from perfect. A variety of factors such as parental influence, relationships with school counselors, and student motivation often influence track placement. At other times, students are placed in the "wrong" track as a result of error. Paula White and her colleagues at the University of Wisconsin at Madison conducted a study of the effects of replacing general-track math courses with college-preparatory math courses in urban high schools with sizable populations of low-achieving students.[20] The selected schools had average achievement in the bottom quartile of schools in their district and in the state. Each school also had a high percentage of students eligible for free and reduced-cost lunches. The authors studied the effects of an implemented "Stretch Regents" course in Rochester, New York, and a University of Chicago Math Project course in Buffalo, New York.

While much of what was learned is of interest to the topic of tracking in general, one aspect of the study is of particular relevance to the question of accelerated learning. The authors found a high degree of track "misplacement" in the Rochester high schools, and were able to use these misplacements for their research purposes—they were able to observe the consequences of placing students of the same similar achievement into different ninth-grade tracks. The authors used logistic regression analysis to determine the effects of ninth-grade track placement on whether or not the student successfully completed math courses in geometry and advanced algebra.

The students' eighth-grade math grades were supposed to be used for track placement, but the researchers found that 39 percent of all students were not placed according to the district track-placement rules. C+ students were supposed to be placed in the Stretch Regents class, a slower-paced class that covered the Regents curriculum. However, the researchers found that if C+ students were downtracked into general math, the chance of completing the two later math courses was 2 percent. If they were placed in the "stretch" class, the chance of completion rose to 23 percent. If they had been misplaced into the regular college class reserved for A and B students, the chance of completing the two-year Regents sequence rose dramatically, to 91 percent. In other words, the low-achieving C+ students had the greatest success if they were accelerated by being placed in a one-year rather than two-year Regents course.

What the studies above indicate is that it is possible to place students, by design or by accident, in an accelerated-learning setting, which results in improved learning for the student without holding back the students who would traditionally be assigned to the class. The two stories that follow show how this can be done successfully on a much larger scale.

PROVIDING THE HIGH-TRACK CURRICULUM
TO ALL STUDENTS

Even as researchers pondered whether it was possible to give the high-track curriculum to all students in detracked classes, without hurting the performance of high achievers, some progressive educators did the work of trying to make that happen. What follows are two stories—one from Israel, the other from suburban New York. In both cases, all students took an accelerated math course—together.

Project TAP (short for Together and Apart), was an attempt to find out whether Israeli junior high schools could better serve the needs of all students by detracking in mathematics.[21] The program integrated whole-class instruction with differentiated support and cooperative learning. The goal of Project TAP was not to bring all students to the same level, but to the highest level possible for each individual child. "Together" signified that students would receive primary instruction in heterogeneous classes and then continue instruction and practice in both heterogeneous and like-ability ("Apart") cooperative groups. To study the effectiveness of the program, TAP classes were compared with traditional tracked classes.

The first part of the study investigated the gap between high and low achievers in the two settings, tracked and untracked. In the tracked setting, the researchers found that the gap between initial low and high achievers expanded over time. In the untracked setting, however, the gap did not expand. Clearly, tracking contributed to a growing gap in achievement.

The second part of the study focused on the gains in achievement in the TAP class. Did the narrowing of the gap come from learning losses of high achievers? The researchers found that it did not. In TAP classes, average and low achievers made significant gains. Although the high achievers in TAP classes showed slightly smaller gains than high achievers in tracked classes, the differences were statistically negligible. Not only did this finding substantiate the effectiveness of TAP classes, it was a clear indictment of tracking: the widening of the gap in tracked classes did not result from high achievers' gains in high-track classes, but rather from the loss in gains of average and lower achievers.

The final part of the study measured teacher attitudes toward teaching in heterogeneous classes. Teachers who received the TAP staff development and support and taught detracked math classes were supportive of the initiative. The researchers concluded that it was possible for all students, including high achievers, to learn math in a mixed-achievement setting and that teaching in such a setting, although challenging, could be supported and enjoyed by their teachers.

The second story of providing all students with an accelerated curriculum is a reform with which I was directly involved. Although the comprehensive detracking reforms of the Rockville Centre School District will be the subject of the next chapter, as an example of how detracking can work for all students when an accelerated curriculum is combined with support for students who struggle, it is worth discussing now.[22]

New York State requires that middle schools provide an unspecified number of students with accelerated instruction in math, allowing students to take an algebra-based course in grade eight. Most middle schools provide this instruction to roughly their top 20 percent of students. Beginning in 1995, after years of study and debate, the superintendent of the Rockville Centre School District, William H. Johnson, and the administration of the middle school, began preparing all sixth-grade students to take algebra in the eighth grade in detracked classes. The district knew that this was going to be more than a mechanical reform. If all students were going to succeed, there would need to be lots of support for students who might struggle, along with professional development support for teachers.

In order to make sure that lower achievers could be successful, the district created support classes that met every other day in addition to the regular class meetings and after-school help four out of five days a week. Teachers were asked what they needed to make the program succeed. The district provided professional development, common planning time, wrote new curriculum, and integrated the use of the calculator in the course, which in the 1990s was not a common practice.

Evaluation of this reform, which I conducted during my doctoral studies, used longitudinal student-achievement data from six student cohorts: the last three sixth-grade cohorts at Rockville Centre's South Side Middle School that were tracked in mathematics and the first three sixth-grade untracked, accelerated cohorts. The performance of the pre- and post-reform groups was compared using an interrupted time series design—that is, results before and after the intervention were compared with other factors being held constant. The study also used demographic data to examine the achievement effects on all groups of students—minority and majority, poor and middle class, as well as low, average, and high achievers. No stone was left unturned in this quest to find out if providing all students with a high-level, accelerated math curriculum in detracked classes was a better strategy.

The first question centered on the long-term benefits from taking an accelerated algebra course in eighth grade. Some who question this strategy claim that lower achievers will "burn out" and stop taking math. Benefit was defined as increased participation in advanced math courses during high school. The study looked at that benefit both overall and on specific student subgroups—black and Latino students, students receiving free or reduced-price lunch, initial low achievers, average achievers, and high achievers. Students' initial level of achievement was determined by their fifth-grade scores on the Math Concepts subtest of the Iowa Test of Basic Skills.

By every measure, students benefited from studying accelerated math in heterogeneously grouped classes. There was a statistically significant increase in the percentages of all students who took advanced math courses in high school, and it applied to every subgroup, including high achievers.

Among students completing trigonometry before they graduated, the percentage of students from low socioeconomic backgrounds increased from 32 to 67 percent; black and Latino students increased from 46 to 67 percent; initial low achievers increased from 38 to 53 percent, average achievers from 81 to 91 percent, and even initial high achievers from 89 to 99 percent. The rates at which each group took pre-calculus and Advanced Placement calculus also increased as well.

Detracking combined with acceleration also helped close the achievement gap associated with poverty. For the trigonometry-based course (New York State Sequential III Mathematics), the advantage gained by members of the universal-acceleration cohort nearly wiped out the disadvantage associated with poverty. For example, students from a low socioeconomic background who participated in the accelerated program had approximately the same probability of completing Sequential III math (0.37) as did students of middle or high socioeconomic backgrounds who attended South Side High School prior to universal acceleration (0.38). Likewise, universal acceleration narrowed the achievement gap associated with being black or Latino.

As noted earlier in this chapter, the most contentious issue in the tracking debate is whether the inclusion of all learners in detracked classes negatively impacts the learning of high-achieving students. This study found that high achievers were not hurt; in fact, they also experienced benefit from detracked eighth-grade math classes. More high achievers—especially those who were black or Latino—took trigonometry, pre-calculus, and Advanced Placement calculus courses in high school. Aside from taking more advanced classes, the math achievement of these students remained high. A careful comparison between high achievers in pre-acceleration and post-acceleration cohorts found that their mean scores on the Sequential I Regents Exam taken in eighth grade were statistically indistinguishable from zero.

Following the achievement gains from detracking eighth-grade mathematics, the Rockville Centre Schools continued detracking at the high school level, producing gains in achievement as measured by the closing of the achievement gap in the earning of the Regents diploma and dramatic increases in the percentages of students taking

International Baccalaureate courses without a decrease in scores or in the performance of higher achievers.[23] That story will be told in the next chapter.

LESSONS LEARNED ABOUT ACHIEVEMENT AND TRACKING

After four decades of research, the pattern that emerged was clear—most studies showed that low-track classes depress student achievement and that the achievement gap between low- and high-achieving students widens over time due to tracking. Readers seeking additional evidence need only look at table 4.1. The numbers are from a study of San Jose, California, schools done by Jeannie Oakes and Kevin Welner. Not only does it show the misplacement of students into the wrong tracks, it also shows that the tracking of students with the same initial achievement affects their learning gains consistently: placement in lower tracks results in fewer learning gains, and even in learning losses over time. The studies in this chapter document this phenomenon over and over again.

Despite all of the studies, some still argue that if the quality of both curriculum and instruction in low-track classes were improved and if more equitable sorting practices were put in place, the negative effects of tracking on low-achieving students could be addressed. The problem is, there is no evidence that this is the case.

The motivation of those seeking to maintain tracking is grounded in the fear that heterogeneous grouping will depress the achievement of highly proficient students—and there is some evidence that if detracking is not carefully done, this could be the case. What seems to matter most in implementing detracking reforms, as we learned in this chapter, is preserving the high-track curriculum, providing teachers with training and professional development in detracking, and ensuring that struggling students receive support.

Yet despite all the evidence of the racial and socioeconomic

Table 4.1

Mathematics Achievement Gains Over Time by Track Level,
Grades 6–12 (San Jose Unified School District, 1985–1992)

INITIAL ACHIEVEMENT LEVEL	INITIAL TRACK PLACEMENT	INITIAL MEAN	AVG. GAIN AFTER 1 YEAR	AVG. GAIN AFTER 2 YEARS	AVG. GAIN AFTER 3 YEARS
20–29	Low	25.4	5.1	7.2	4.7
	Std	25.1	8.7	16.5	10.5
30–39	Low	34.8	–0.1	0.8	–0.2
	Std	34.8	3.5	6.7	5.0
40–49	Low	44.5	–1.2	0.8	–1.2
	Std	44.9	0.2	4.5	5.2
50–59	Low	54.4	–2.2	–1.9	–1.9
	Std	54.6	0.1	3.7	3.8
	Acc	55.4	6.5	11.9	9.6
60–69	Low	64.4	–3.8	–0.1	–2.3
	Std	64.3	–0.7	3.7	3.8
	Acc	65.4	5.7	8.4	7.6
70–79	Low	73.4	–2.9	–2.1	–
	Std	74.2	–2.4	–0.9	–1.0
	Acc	74.9	4.4	7.8	7.6
80–89	Low	83.5	–16.0	–	–
	Std	83.7	–4.2	–5.4	–3.1
	Acc	85.0	0.2	2.3	2.6

stratification perpetuated by tracking, inequitable track-placement practices, and depressed achievement for all but the most advanced students, tracking continues. There are, however, schools that, with determination and careful planning, have managed to detrack despite the odds, and students are reaping the rewards. The next chapter tells one such story.

5

The District That
Stopped Sorting Students

Rockville Centre

In many ways, the suburban community of Rockville Centre, on Long Island, New York, was an unlikely place for a detracking reform. Although the school district had been under a court order to desegregate in 1977, the order applied to the elementary school level, where no tracking system was in place. Closing one school and rezoning a few others solved the problem to the satisfaction of the court. The district's overall scores were competitive, and there were few complaints about the status quo.

What was not readily apparent, however, was the sizable achievement gap between the majority of students, who were from white, upper-middle-class households, and the 21 percent of district students who were African American or Latino. Most of the school's minority students came from households with relatively low incomes—the majority being eligible for free or reduced-price lunch. Tucked away above the boutiques and restaurants of downtown Rockville Centre was Section 8 subsidized housing. And behind a strip mall sat a housing project on the outskirts of downtown.

The achievement gap was something that School Superintendent William H. Johnson was determined to change.[1] He was especially concerned about a thirty-point gap that existed between white and minority students in the earning of the New York State Regents diploma, the diploma designed to indicate that students were prepared for college.

Bill Johnson was drawn to equity reform. He began his career in education in Bridgeport, Connecticut, teaching kids no one else wanted to teach—special education students with severe emotional disabilities. After his first year in the classroom, he concluded that the students in his class did not belong there—separate and apart from the rest of the school. It was made clear to him, however, that the school did not want these students mainstreamed. Johnson felt strongly that his students' deficits related to their behavior, not their ability to learn, and he tried to convince school administrators that his students should be taught in regular classes and taken out only for periods of special help. The teachers that he worked with were not receptive; in fact, they were hostile to Johnson's efforts.

When he went to Teachers College, Columbia University, for his doctoral studies, Johnson's convictions about mainstreaming only became stronger. He started teaching at Fairfield University and consulting on Long Island, trying to get others to buy into the concept of a more normalized education for special needs students, in which special education services were used as resources, rather than to separate and isolate students.

In 1979 he joined the Rockville Centre School District as director of special education. He served in various roles as an assistant superintendent both for instruction and for business, and in 1986 he was appointed superintendent of schools, a position he continues to hold today.

In 1981, several years prior to his becoming superintendent, racial tensions broke out among Rockville Centre's South Side High School students. There were riots between white students from blue-collar homes and black students from the housing project. What the students involved had in common was that they were nearly all in the high school's low-track classes. Bill Johnson made the connection between tracking and racial tensions. When he became superintendent he knew what needed to be done—the low-track classes had to go. He hired a middle school principal, Larry Vandewater, and an assistant principal, Delia Garrity, who shared his passion for equity. He hired a high school principal, Robin Calitri, who had been a teacher of low-track classes in a low-SES district and understood the problems inherent in tracking. Together they began to dismantle the tracking system by eliminating the low-track classes and consolidating tracks.

REDUCING THE TRACKS

Each core academic area in the Rockville Centre middle and high schools had at least two tracks, and in some cases as many as five. Students had a different educational experience depending on the track in which they were placed. Minority students, especially those who received free or reduced-price lunch, were greatly overrepresented in the low-track classes and largely absent from the upper tracks.

In 1989, under Bill Johnson and his team, detracking reform was implemented in the middle school for English and social studies classes. Gradually, five tracks were consolidated into one. It was a great success—the number of students failing courses decreased, even though it was the lower-aptitude courses that were being eliminated. Slowly and surely, the middle school continued the work—eliminating the lower track, with students "leveling up" to the higher track. Principal Larry Vandewater placed the reform within the context of his philosophy of middle school.[2] He would remind parents that middle school was not a mini high school. He emphasized the importance of meeting the unique social and emotional needs of children as they entered the teenage years. This was a time to expand opportunity, not restrict it. Vandewater explained how having all students together in student-centered classes was an important feature of a good middle school program. Slowly and surely, over the span of five years, tracks disappeared. Soon only math and science remained tracked, with two levels in each subject.

During that time, in the fall of 1991, racial tensions again erupted at South Side High School. Over a period of two weeks a series of racial incidents, including a fight, roiled the school, catching the attention of Long Island's leading newspaper, *Newsday*, and raising concerns within the community at large.

High school principal Robin Calitri knew that the clustering of students in unchallenging, low-track classes was a root cause of the problem. He worked with Bill Johnson to establish an ambitious goal—by the year 2000, 75 percent of all South Side High School students would graduate with a Regents diploma. There was only one way to achieve that goal: the non-Regents, low-track classes would have to go. A new policy was put in place. There would be only two tracks at every level—Regents and honors—and it was up to students and families to make the choice about which class to take. According to Calitri, the elimination of the low track and the establishment of choice had to go hand in hand. He knew that some parents would fear the sudden influx of students from the low track into the Regents classes. Those who did could have their children opt in to honors.

Not only did the addition of choice make the elimination of the low track politically feasible, it expanded the number of students who took honors courses in grades nine and ten, and the school's elite International Baccalaureate courses in grades eleven and twelve.

The IB Diploma Program, which is offered in the final two years of secondary school, is a rigorous course of study that encompasses six areas of curriculum. Participating schools must be accredited by the International Baccalaureate Organization (IBO). Due to the demanding nature of the IB curriculum and assessments, colleges recognize the rigor of the program, and so students may earn college credit for IB coursework in a manner consistent with the earning of AP credit.

When Bill Johnson was the district's director of special education, he brought the IB program in as a gifted program. Students can participate in the program in one of two ways—they can take individual courses, or elect a more demanding level of participation by becoming an IB diploma candidate. To earn the diploma, they must take the courses needed to earn a minimum of twenty-four points on assessments from six IB courses, and complete the three so-called central elements: a chronicle of their extracurricular/service learning activities (known as CAS, which stands for Creativity, Action, Service); a transdisciplinary epistemology course (Theory of Knowledge); and an extensive independent research project (the extended essay), which they work on over the course of two years under the guidance of a faculty mentor.

In 1988, only nine South Side High School students were candidates for the International Baccalaureate diploma. By 1998, due to the open-door policy to the honors track, there were eighty-eight IB diploma candidates, and more than one-third of all students were taking at least one IB course. As the school continued to detrack, that percentage would rise even further.

ACCELERATING ALL STUDENTS IN MATHEMATICS

Even as these changes were occurring in the high school, the middle school was extending detracking into math and science. Johnson and Calitri had decided that it was time to prepare additional students for advanced math and science so that more students could enter the high school's International Baccalaureate program. At that time, only two of the ten eighth-grade sections were accelerated in math, which meant that only about fifty students had the opportunity to take algebra (then called Sequential Mathematics I) in eighth grade.

Vandewater and Garrity enthusiastically supported the change. They disagreed with the "limited seat" approach previously endorsed by the mathematics departments and used the high school principal's request as a rationale to extend opportunity to more students.

Rather than having an enrollment limit, the accelerated class would now be open to any student who met the selection criterion (performance on a test designed by middle school teachers), even if sections needed to be added to accommodate students.

Although more students were now taking the course, scores on the Regents exam were excellent, and it became apparent to school administrators that, given the opportunity, students previously placed in lower tracks were capable of accelerating in math. As the high school was opening honors to student and family choice, the middle school decided that students and their families would be the final decision-makers regarding enrollment in accelerated middle school courses. From 1992 until 1995, between 33 percent and 42 percent of students opted to take high-track mathematics and science.

But there was still work to be done. Although accelerated math was now theoretically available to all students, in practice white, African American, Asian, and Latino students were making the choice to accelerate at different rates. For example, during the 1996–97 school year, only 11 percent of African American students and 15 percent of Latino students were accelerated in eighth-grade math, while the overall acceleration rate for white and Asian students was 50 percent. The district's upper-middle-class students were choosing to accelerate at greater rates, and the pre-algebra, eighth-grade math classes began to assume the racial and socioeconomic stratification of low-track classes. Not only were minority students overrepresented in the less demanding classes, failure rates in the lower track were higher, and student motivation was lower. The dynamics described in chapter 3 were playing out in South Side Middle School, despite the best efforts of school administrators to create a more equitable learning environment.

Choice, then, was not the solution. There was only one strategy that would work to truly serve all students and close the achievement gap—every student had to be accelerated in math, and all student tracking in science had to be eliminated.[3] The district developed a multiyear plan to remove the less challenging math option, thereby eliminating all curricular stratification in middle-school mathematics and science. Heterogeneous, accelerated math classes were set to begin with the sixth-grade class entering the middle school in the fall of 1995.

When Bill Johnson and Assistant Principal Delia Garrity met with the middle school math teachers to inform them of the change, there was dissent. Some teachers wanted the revised curriculum to begin in the elementary schools, which would have postponed for several years acceleration at the middle school level. Garrity, a former mathematics teacher, strongly believed that such a delay was unnecessary, and implementation began, despite teacher reservations, with the incoming sixth-grade class.

When the change was first introduced, parents and teachers worried that there would not be enough support for struggling math students, and that high achievers would be shortchanged when placed in a class with students previously tracked as lower performers. In order to address the first concern, every-other-day math "workshops" were added to provide help to students who needed it.

In addition, the math teachers at each grade level were given a common planning period in which to develop lessons and assessments.[4] This allowed them to plan their regular and workshop classes together, and gave them opportunities to discuss how to meet the needs of all students. In this way, teachers were able to work together and support one another in creating assessments and analyzing student results.

Not surprisingly, the parents of high-achieving students were concerned that their children might not be as challenged as they had been under the former system. The administration assured them that the curriculum had not been changed or "watered down" in any way.

The teachers provided voluntary enrichment activities, both during and after school, for those students seeking extra challenge. High achievers could also participate in competitive organizations such as the Mathletes program. The first cohort of students detracked in mathematics included the children of the assistant principal and board of education members. Their presence in the class sent a powerful message to the community that the school had confidence in the new, more equitable math program.

Staff development needs were also of concern. The assistant principal was active throughout the implementation phase, attending all faculty meetings and providing feedback on student progress. Garrity carefully analyzed the pass/fail rate of students each quarter and shared this information with the teachers. This was a key strategy in addressing concerns that the program was not working. Although teachers had expected failure rates to increase, the opposite occurred. Low-achieving students appeared to be more successful in heterogeneously grouped, accelerated classes with a more demanding curriculum. Despite the encouraging data, however, a few teachers continued to doubt that acceleration was in the best interest of all students.

The principal and assistant principal were careful to engage those faculty members who were critical of the new math program, talking out points raised and addressing the issues. Their response was always to ask what more was needed for success. By doing so, they skillfully moved the discussion from "Is this reform working?" to "What do we need to make it work?"

When schools detrack, dissenting teachers align themselves with dissenting parents. That is what occurred in Rockville Centre in 1998, just prior to when the eighth grade sat for the Regents exam. Passing rates in math began to decrease to pre-detracking levels. The board of education informed the superintendent that parents were expressing concerns about large numbers of students failing the Regents examination. In addition, one of the school's math teachers was apparently telling parents that acceleration was not working for average and low achievers.

Bill Johnson arrived at the school during the teachers' common planning period and asked to meet with them. After complimenting them on their reform efforts, Johnson told them of a "rumor" that was circulating in the school community that the detracking initiative was not working. He told the teachers that he hoped they had not "written off kids," and asked what resources or help they needed to ensure that students would be successful. By asking teachers what they needed, he steered the discussion away from a political battle and back to the work at hand. The teacher who was badmouthing the detracking reform was not directly confronted, but the whisper campaign did not continue. She got the message that her "behind the scenes" attempts to end math detracking were doing the school community, and the district's students, a disservice.

When it came time to take the test, the students did well. The eighth-grade passing rate on the Sequential I Mathematics Regents was higher than the teacher-assigned passing rates for the eighth-grade marking periods. More than 84 percent passed the exam, and 52 percent were at the mastery level with a score of 85 percent or above. The passing rate continued to improve, so that since 2011 about 97 percent of all of the eighth-graders pass this exam, which is a New York State graduation standard.[5] The following year, eighth-grade science was detracked. No tracking currently exists at South Side Middle School. All students study an accelerated and enriched course of studies together.

DETRACKING SOUTH SIDE HIGH SCHOOL

When I arrived at South Side High School in the spring of 1997 as an assistant principal, tracking had been reduced to two, and in a few cases three, levels or options in each subject area. The one exception was foreign language, in which there was only one level in grades nine through twelve.

That level of detracking had attracted me to the school. I had become an administrator because the high school in the district where

I taught was heavily tracked, with each track racially identifiable. The more the school became diverse, the more it tracked. As much as I loved teaching, I was ethically uncomfortable with the tracking system and felt that I could not remain. When I interviewed with principal Robin Calitri, I met another educator who understood the problems associated with tracking and had the courage to tackle them head-on.

The fall after I arrived, the first math-accelerated cohort entered the high school. As mentioned above, there were some teachers who had quietly attempted to undermine the detracking initiative. One of the ways they tried to do so was with respect to special education students. The middle school fully includes special education students, with the exception of developmentally delayed students (for example, students with Down syndrome, who are in a Life Skills Program).

Even though the special education students are fully included, the classroom teachers were treating them differently in math. They were sure that the students could not handle the rigors of algebra in eighth grade, so without the knowledge or permission of the middle school administration, they were giving some of the students different worksheets and exams. When it came time to take the Regents exam, they admitted that these students were not prepared to take the test and would have to repeat the course in high school.

In the last chapter, I told the story of how, despite all of the resources we could muster, we could not make that low-track class work. I don't know why I thought we could beat the odds, especially given my commitment to detracking. I learned the very valuable lesson that heterogeneous grouping is a far better strategy than just adding additional resources for meeting the needs of struggling learners. During the second year of accelerated math at South Side Middle School, all of the special education students in the eighth grade were prepared to take the test and never again did we adopt a low-track solution.

In addition to supervising the math and science departments at the high school, I was in charge of the review of the school's midterm and final exams. As I reviewed the school's English and social studies exams for ninth graders, I noticed that although the tests were the same for regular and honors classes, the honors students' grades on the test became part of a weighted average. My first response was that this was unfair—upon further reflection, I questioned why we needed two levels of study at all. If the cumulative exams were the same, how different could the courses really be? I discussed my observations with teacher leaders and the rest of the administrative team, and Robin Calitri agreed. The next year there was only one level of English and social studies for ninth graders, with an honors-by-application option. The following year, the honors activities were infused into the courses so that there was one common educational experience for all.

Robin Calitri retired in 2000, after more than a decade of reducing tracking and opening the doors of advanced courses to more and more students. He had become an outspoken leader of detracking on Long Island, inspiring others to question the status quo and follow his lead. Stepping up to become principal, I was very proud to continue along the path of providing equitable and excellent learning experiences to more students through detracking.

Despite the reduction in tracking, there was still a big gap in the earning of the Regents diploma at South Side High School in the year 2000. For those students who entered South Side in 1996 (the graduating class of 2000), only 32 percent of African American and Hispanic graduates earned Regents diplomas, as opposed to 88 percent of white and Asian American graduates. Getting rid of the non-Regents track was not enough—minority students were not passing the tests required for earning the college-prep diploma at the same rate as the majority students. Because New York State intended to eliminate the local diploma option in a few years, this was a serious problem.[6]

We were also able to observe the effects of detracking in grade nine English and social studies. Compared with the lower-track ninth-grade English and social studies classes, the new heterogeneous classes had fewer discipline problems and the tone and culture of the classes were similar to the former honors classes. The teachers kept expectations for student performance high, and modified teaching strategies, not standards and curriculum. They integrated student portfolios to give students more personalized feedback, and employed a cooperative, "jigsaw" approach in which activities were assigned that were appropriate for the learner. Students might have different passages to read or different tasks to complete as part of an overarching assignment tackled by the jigsaw group, composed of members assigned to the different tasks. Teachers began teaching the same books at the same time so that support classes could truly support the curriculum, rather than focusing exclusively on skills development. When the heterogeneous classes proved successful, we decided to move the model forward.

In 2000, the New York State science course in biology was redeveloped as a course called The Living Environment. We used the rewriting of the curriculum as an opportunity to detrack and have all students take the same course. The following year we detracked mathematics. Each time, we wrote a support curriculum along with the class curriculum. While teachers still had their own styles, they were expected to be on the same topics to ensure that the support classes were able to pre- and post-teach curriculum. Because there were no tracks in foreign language, tracking having been abandoned in those courses in the 1980s, the ninth-grade class that entered the high school in 2001 was the first class to be heterogeneously grouped in all subjects.

Each time we moved forward, students were more successful at passing Regents exams. We began to explore how we could prepare all students for the best curriculum that we had to offer—the International Baccalaureate courses taught in grades eleven and twelve. Central and building administration agreed that the time had come to give all tenth-grade students the honors curriculum in English and social studies.

The English teachers were onboard with the change, but there was some hesitation among veteran social studies teachers. Many enjoyed teaching the honors class, and they worried that top students would be shortchanged. They also worried that without the test-prep focus of the lower track, lower-achieving students might do poorly on the tenth-grade Regents exam in social studies.

I met with the department and shared some data I thought they would find interesting. I put student names, ninth-grade final averages, social studies track, and tenth-grade Regents scores on a spreadsheet. I then matched students who had the same final averages in social studies in ninth grade, but were in different tenth-grade tracks. A clear pattern emerged. If students were in the tenth-grade honors track, their Regents exam scores were higher than the corresponding student who had the same ninth-grade final average but was in the lower track.

The teachers understood what the data indicated, and became more comfortable with the change. I told them that while the decision was made by administration to change the program, they would be in charge of revising the curriculum and materials to meet the needs of all students—higher and lower achievers alike.

All was going well within the departments, and teachers were onboard for the change. When it came time, however, to make a presentation to the board of education, all hell broke loose. Unknown to us, a parent who was active in the PTA and quietly opposed detracking had emailed parents far and wide. When the meeting began, we were greeted by an indignant audience. For hours, the teachers and I answered question after question posed by parents who feared that rigor would be eliminated, or that the course would be too difficult for some. Although parents were polite and somewhat restrained, coded comments regarding the learning potential of some students became part of the dialogue. One parent argued that some students were destined to work in the mailroom and that being in an honors class was not for them. At one point, another parent argued that rather than detrack, we should just "raise the ceiling in the low-track class." John Murphy, who was the teacher facilitator of our IB program, responded, "This is not about raising ceilings for some students. This is about ripping the ceiling off for everyone." It was the perfect, sincere response.

For several hours, we continued to present our findings and provide reassurance. We showed data that demonstrated how results had always gone up with detracking, while top scores had not gone down. We spoke of our support classes and how they would fill the learning gaps for struggling students. We explained that we would create grading systems that rewarded student effort, so that every student could be successful. Finally, we discussed our commitment to academic challenge, assuring parents that the goals of the curriculum would not be lowered.

We left the meeting tired, concerned, and unsure of the position of the board. After the meeting, the board grappled with the decision, and to members' credit they supported the recommendation and the change moved forward.

The teachers took great care to ensure that the curricula for the new tenth-grade courses were rigorous and enriched. Delia Garrity, who was by then the assistant superintendent for curriculum and instruction, brought in a consultant to help with curriculum development. In tenth-grade English classes, teachers integrated the use of the IB Commentary (a detailed, coherent literary interpretation of a brief passage or poem), and in the social studies classes, they integrated the beginnings of the IB Historical Investigation (an internally assessed component of the course whereby students create an annotated bibliography based on a research question of their own making). Teachers also developed process and product rubrics to assess individual student growth.

Tenth-grade English language arts (ELA) support classes were transformed from a remedial model into classes focused on the accelerated content learned by all students, using a pre- and post-teaching approach for struggling learners. All students were given the opportunity to take this every-other-day support class, and approximately 15 percent of students entered the support class. Tenth-grade English teachers agreed to teach the same literature at the same time so that the support classes could truly pre-teach content. Social studies teachers communicated regularly with the teachers of the ELA support classes so that the ELA teachers could assist the social studies students in the writing of essays. We worked hard to prove our critics wrong, and it worked. Detracking in tenth-grade English and social studies was a great success. Parents who were opposed to the change later praised the across-the-board implementation of the advanced curriculum. One parent, who had been concerned that the newly detracked English course would be too difficult for her daughter, told the board about the wonderful dinnertime conversations she began having with her child about the books she was reading in class. No parent of former "high-track students" complained that their child was not being sufficiently challenged. By working hard on implementation, our teachers created seamless change and assured detracking's success.

Beginning in the 2004 school year, our tenth-grade math course, in advanced algebra and trigonometry, was detracked, with an every-other-day support or enrichment (advanced topics) option available to students who wanted more instruction. In September 2006, the last vestige of tracking in the tenth grade was eliminated, when the chemistry teachers asked if we could detrack chemistry, blending honors and Regents. Finally, in grades nine and ten, there was one course of rigorous study for all students in all subjects.

Detracking was far more than a mechanical process of eliminating tracks and rewriting curriculum. Every teacher went through six hours of training in differentiated instruction. Two master teachers and I taught the course. We wanted to make sure that our teachers knew to differentiate methodology, not curriculum. Teachers were trained in the use of jigsaw techniques, utilizing the multiple intelligences of our students to facilitate instruction, and in differentiating assessments so that students could show what they know.

During faculty meetings, there were short presentations on how to individualize questions and increase student involvement in lessons. Since 2005, teachers have participated each year in lesson study so that they can collegially practice their teaching—always with purpose and always focusing on the learner.

Special education teachers were trained not only in co-teaching but in how to take field notes on student learning. Using those notes, they are able to give feedback to the general education teacher on what students are learning, and the notes guide their instruction in special education support classes.

All of the above had a positive effect on student achievement. By the time the detracked classes moved through the school, the gap between the rate at which our majority and minority students earned the Regents diploma rate had closed (see figure 5.1).

Figure 5.1
Growth in Attainment of the Regents Diploma:
Graduates of the Class of 2000 Compared with the Class of 2009

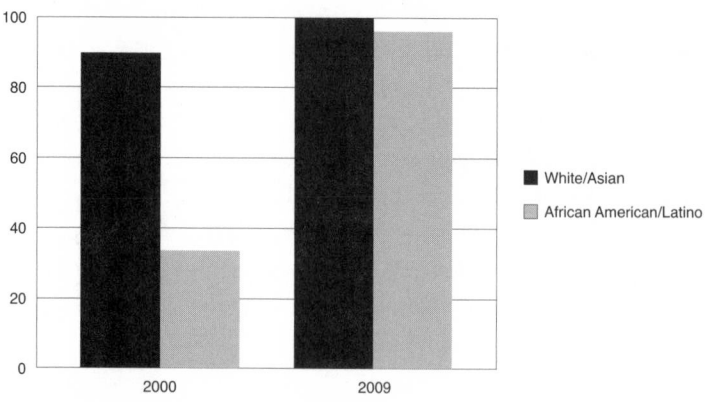

Even though, due to changes in diploma requirements, Regents rates across the state had risen, the rates for South Side High School students clearly exceeded the average rates for New York State students. Only 45 percent of Hispanic and 43 percent of black students who entered high school in 2004 in New York graduated four years later with a Regents diploma. The rate for South Side High School Hispanic and black students who graduated with a Regents diploma in four years was nearly 90 percent. In addition, nearly half of the minority members of that cohort graduated with a Regents Diploma with Advanced Designation, approximately the same rate as the cohort rate for white students in the state of New York. In order to graduate with Advanced Designation, students have to pass additional math Regents exams in geometry and advanced algebra and trigonometry, as well as in an additional science. Clearly, detracking was having a positive effect on closing South Side High School's achievement gap.

DETRACKING AND THE INTERNATIONAL BACCALAUREATE

Because we believed that the curriculum for the best student was the best curriculum for all, we looked to the International Baccalaureate to guide our program. It is a high-quality curriculum, with assessments embedded throughout the course. We also knew from our graduates that it prepared them well for college. We conducted two studies, which interviewed graduates or their parents regarding college completion. What we found was that if students took two IB courses—one in English and one in math—their chances of graduating from college in four years dramatically increased. The four-year college graduation rate for such students was 90 percent.

The structure and philosophy underlying the IB Diploma program was also an ideal fit for the school district's detracking reform initiatives. Both the school district and the International Baccalaureate Program believe that "student capability . . . is not a static, invariant quality, such as a student's height would be, but is something more dynamic and variable in nature."[7] That, of course, is the belief on which our detracking reform was founded. Both the school, and the IB as an organization, understood that given the opportunity to study enriched, challenging curriculum that develops higher-order thinking skills, student capacity to learn and think can grow and expand. Although not everyone may get to the same place, given the opportunity, and with skilled teachers, students can learn far more in detracked classes with a challenging curriculum than they can when they are isolated from higher-achieving peers in the low track.

As the high school progressively detracked grades nine and ten, enrollment in eleventh- and twelfth-grade IB courses grew. The number of students pursuing the full IB diploma increased as well. Even after a decade of an open-door policy for IB study, only 27 percent of students who entered the ninth grade at South Side High School in 1997 (the year prior to universal acceleration in mathematics) were IB diploma candidates. In contrast, 44 percent of students who began South Side in 2003 graduated as IB diploma candidates. In each subsequent year, that proportion has been met or exceeded. In 2012, 45 percent were IB diploma candidates and 34 percent of the entire class earned the IB diploma.

Even if students did not pursue the IB diploma, the increase in students participating in IB courses soared. Figure 5.2 shows the increase in the numbers of students who took IB math and IB English, courses that the school had established were linked to later college success. By 2009, nearly all students were graduating having taken those courses—a far cry from the numbers just a decade before.

At the same time, the scores of students taking the exam did not decline. For example, in 2000, 40 percent of the graduating class took IB English. The average score was 4.5 (IB scores range from 1 to 7). However, as the proportion of students who took the course grew, the average remained remarkably stable. Ten years later, in 2010, when over 70 percent of the class was taking the exam, the average score was 4.45. The same stability in scores occurred in IB math courses.

Figure 5.2
*Percentage of South Side High School Graduating Class Taking
IB English and an IB Math Course: 1998–2009*

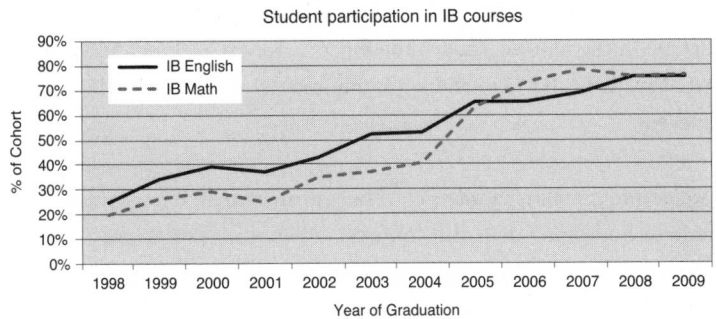

The stability of scores was a clear indication that opening the gates of opportunity to more students did not have a negative impact on learning. In addition, it also provided evidence that the heterogeneous classes in grades nine and ten, which were designed to prepare students for rigorous learning in IB courses, were doing their job. The school had leveled up without watering down.

In the fall of 2011, all eleventh-grade students took IB English. The Regents track was gone. That year, South Side High School's eleventh-grade Regents results were the best ever. Only one student, who was an English-language learner (ELL) with a learning disabilty, did not pass the test. The average score on the state exam was 88 percent, and 90 percent of all students met the New York State college readiness score of 75 percent. Detracking had once again made a difference.

In the fall of 2013, for the first time, all students took the IB English course in detracked classes in twelfth grade. Although families would be allowed to decide whether their students took the exam (which allowed students to receive weighted grades), nearly 90 percent decided to do so. There is now one challenging course in English language arts K–12 in Rockville Centre Public Schools.

LESSONS LEARNED

The Rockville Centre Schools presents a remarkable case study of detracking reform—not only in terms of student achievement but in the success of the district in moving the reform forward. In a 2006 article in the journal *Theory into Practice*, Kevin Welner and I discuss what we believed were the key components of the Rockville Centre success.[8]

Stable and committed leadership. The reform benefited from the leadership of Superintendent Bill Johnson, a veteran of more than twenty years in the district. His core beliefs in equity and in excellence guided the detracking effort, and during his tenure, he appointed principals and assistants who shared them. Bill understood that although the district could help teachers improve their teaching skills, if they did not believe in the mission of the district—equity and excellence for all students—they could not be successful in Rockville Centre. He always included questions to tease out candidates' beliefs when he hired teachers and administrators alike. My own belief that the work we were doing was so important and gratifying solidified my commitment to the principalship.

Elimination of the lowest track first. The research is clear—low-track classes depress student achievement and cause students to fall further and further behind. When low tracks are eliminated, there is a bump-up of achievement and an improvement in school culture. Teachers who teach low-track classes are rarely sorry to see them go. However, there is a more important reason to eliminate the low track first. They are, in demographically diverse schools, the most racially isolated. When you examine the evidence of how students fall further and further behind, as presented in table 4.1, it is clearly the track that does the most harm.

A gradual approach to creating heterogeneous classes. The first step in this process was parental choice. As more families chose the upper track, the class became more heterogeneous in skill (though not demography) over time. This allowed teachers to adjust to the change gradually and expand their teaching repertoire. They were ready when it became time to abolish the last vestiges of tracking.

By the time the schools moved to a one-track system, the transition to heterogeneity was smooth. It is critical to keep in mind, however, that choice alone is not an effective strategy in creating heterogeneous classes, and must be considered an interim step only— choice by itself will not eliminate the stratification patterns resulting from students being assigned to tracks based on selection criteria.

Support for struggling learners. Schools cannot expect to teach a high-track curriculum to all without buidling in the proper support for students who struggle. Support classes, extra help, peer tutoring, and other such measures were a critical part of Rockville Centre's detracking success. National Honor Society members were obligated to provide turoring as part of their service. This occurred both during the school day during free periods and after school.

Steady, determined progress. The school did not wait for everyone to "get ready to get ready to get ready." When math teachers argued that accelerated math needed to begin in kindergarten, the district wisely disagreed. That said, the process of detracking was gradual and thoughtful. For example, it was only after IB English 11 for all students was in place for two years that the reform moved to grade twelve. This was to make sure that students were adequately prepared for IB English 12 after taking the eleventh-grade detracked class. When there was data to suggest that the change was effective, the district moved on.

Collection and dissemination of achievement data. The tracking debate is an emotional one. Parents have reasonable concerns when the status quo is challenged. They want the best for their children. Anecdotal evidence is brought to the table about why tracking should continue and why it should be abandoned. When the conversation focuses on data, some of the "heat" leaves the argument. During the debate at the school board meeting described in this chapter, it was helpful for me to have my charts on hand to show that previous detracking efforts had not resulted in a decline in student performance—both overall and for high-performing students.

Careful selection and retention of staff. There are teachers who remain convinced that tracking systems benefit students. With time and support, teaching skills can be enhanced, and beliefs can change based on individual experience; however, it makes sense, for schools committed to detracking reforms, that all teachers have an open mind when it comes to this issue. This is something that can be established during the hiring and probationary processes. Teachers who are resistant to detracking reforms are not a good match for schools attempting such reforms.

Methodological creation of heterogeneous classes. Even when schools enact detracking reforms, there can be de facto tracking that occurs in high schools as a result of the vagrancies of the master schedule. For example, music classes or ELL classes can cluster students into certain sections. That is terribly unfair to teachers. Both South Side Middle School and South Side High School meticulously balance sections so that each has its fair share of both high and low achievers.

Responding to parental concerns. Parents' concerns cannot be dismissed. Parents love their children and naturally put their own child's needs first. It is critical that the school have a plan to meet the needs of every child in heterogeneous classes. Teachers need strategies to challenge high achievers, and the needs of lower achievers must also be met. School leaders need to be prepared with a plan on how such differentiation should be accomplished. Support classes, mandatory extra help, and peer tutors are a few effective strategies. In our tenth grade, students who wanted greater challenge could "opt in" for an extra period of advanced instruction in chemistry, take the every-other-day supplementary course in advanced algebra to study advanced topics, and in grades nine through twelve take science research. This was in addition to a curriculum that was rigorous and many opportunities for students to participate in honor societies and academic competitions.

Support for and engagement of staff. Asking teachers to teach in a newly detracked school is, at least initally, asking a lot. Teachers deserve professional development, support in the creation of curriculum, and praise for their efforts. This is not to say that teachers or a committee need to be the decision makers regarding tracking. That is a decision for school leaders to make. However, they do have a right to know why the school is detracking, to understand and review the data, to feel supported, and to have a voice in the process. Delia Garrity wisely asked the math teachers, "What do you need to make this work?" Teachers were actively engaged in curriculum building, curriculum critique, and choice of materials.

In the next two chapters I will discuss other schools that detracked—to greater and lesser extents. Rockville Centre offers a successful account of detracking. Although the stories that follow are different, they are also remarkably similar with respect to the results the schools sought and the challenges they faced.

6

The Politics of Detracking
When Equity and Fear Collide

The Rockville Centre Schools' experience with detracking illustrates just how powerful detracking can be in providing a challenging and equitable educational experience for all students. Given what we know about the racial and socioeconomic stratification associated with tracking, and the evidence regarding its negative effects on the achievement of low-track students, the reader might assume that detracking reforms have been widely enacted during the past two decades. This is not the case: in fact, tracking is alive and well. Although there has been some reduction in its utilization, it is still very much a part of American schooling. In many regards, Rockville Centre is one of the few examples of a successfully detracked school system.

The reason for its continuance is that many school leaders who begin to detrack their schools feel as though they have walked into a political minefield. Detracking, even when it is done as a "leveling up" process ensuring that high achievers are not harmed (as it was designed in Rockville Centre), is highly controversial and meets with significant resistance.[1] It evokes strong emotional responses regarding beliefs about intelligence, race, class, entitlement, privilege, and merit. These beliefs intersect with vested interests, resulting in alliances among parent groups and sometimes teachers.

FACTORS INHIBITING DETRACKING REFORMS

Kevin Welner has characterized the barriers to detracking as both normative and political.[2] The normative barriers derive from deep-seated beliefs about the interplay between IQ or "ability" and merit. Those who would detrack encounter beliefs about the purpose of schooling for "different types of kids," as well as ideas about for whom schooling is really intended. The long-held and jealously guarded belief systems about fixed intelligence, merit, and entitlement are part of the normative barriers that must be challenged and overcome.

The political barriers are prodigious as well. The fiercest political opponents of detracking are almost always the parents of high-track students. The system rewards those students (and by proxy their parents) with status and recognition. These are the students who "do school" well. Because they do, they believe that they have earned the privilege to have classes designed for them—the "purple tie" of recognition—and, although it is rarely said, access to the best teachers in the school.

Well-educated parents, as we learned in the previous chapter, understand the significance of high-track classes on the college transcript, and so they are particularly adept at making sure that their children are placed in such classes. They are also skilled and confident speakers at school board meetings. How they influence the politics of schools on the issue of detracking will be further discussed below and in future chapters.

Jeannie Oakes and her team of researchers spent years studying schools that were undergoing detracking reforms. One three-year case study of ten districts provides a plethora of information regarding why detracking is so difficult to undertake.[3] In my interviews for this book of those who had embarked on detracking reforms, I saw that the same patterns of resistance were encountered over and over again. These patterns are summarized below, and thus will provide a lens through which to interpret the case studies in subsequent chapters. Those chapters will recount stories of detracking efforts that met with various levels of success. First, however, it is important to ground the reader in what researchers learned from studying the earliest attempts at detracking. Five major factors have been found to work in concert in inhibiting or derailing detracking reforms.

Unidimensional View of Human Intelligence

Oakes and her team discovered that those who favored tracking view intelligence as something one is born with and that is fixed at birth. They believed intelligence to be unidimensional—that is, they do not subscribe to the view of Howard Gardner and others that there are multiple intelligences that students possess and that it is valuable for schools to tap into them when teaching students.[4]

For those who believe that intelligence has one dimension, being "smart" is most often associated with the speed at which one retains and comprehends information. Interestingly enough, both of these skills, retention and comprehension, are considered to be lower-level thinking skills on Bloom's Taxonomy of the Cognitive Domain, a classification of learning objectives first put forward in 1956 by educators led by Benjamin Bloom and still in use today. Nevertheless, a student's ability to retain and comprehend information is easy to quantify and thus becomes what appears to be an objective measure of intelligence. For those who believe in the unidimensional view, each person's intelligence can be plotted on a normal curve.

This view of intelligence is based on the belief that intelligence is fixed by the time a student enters school. Therefore, parents demand that schools differentiate programs and tailor them to the speed of learning that is associated with bands of intelligence and performance. Most of the pressure for this differentiation (which leads to tracking) comes from the parents of the most proficient students. Jeannie Oakes met the stiffest resistance to her detracking research from the advocates of "gifted" students. Because the traditional view of intelligence favors such students, the maintenance of tracking becomes a cause célèbre.

Stereotypical Beliefs About Race, Class, and Learning

In 1990, I was a middle school teacher of Spanish in the Lawrence Public Schools on Long Island. Our seventh-grade program was heterogeneously grouped, followed by a three-track program of instruction that began in grade eight. At a parent-teacher conference, a father leaned over the desk in which he was sitting and forcefully said, "Put my daughter in honors next year. I do not want her in the class with the black kids." I was shocked and horrified and politely made it clear that his remark was inappropriate and offensive. I have never forgotten that moment. It was the first time I realized just how intertwined race and tracking were.

Most people are not as crude as that father was. They are far more skillful at coding their race-based objections. Oakes and her team found ample evidence of stereotypical beliefs used to justify the obvious stratification that results from tracking.[5] Some teachers openly made remarks that expressed their beliefs that black, Latino, and Native American children had a limited capacity to learn. They would define what a good student does, and then make excuses, based in culture, for why minority students were not capable of being good students. Much of what they described as being a good student was based on compliance and behavior—what is often termed "the school-ready child."

Parents of high-track students often use that description to code racial stereotypes, replacing race concerns with concerns about "behavior" that would disrupt the classroom routine and thus their child's education. This was true in Woodland Hills, Pennsylvania (which will be discussed later in greater detail), where parents often expressed their concern that disruptive students would take away from the learning of others.

As we detracked the tenth-grade English and social studies program at our high school in Rockville Centre, one parent called me and expressed her concern that tenth grade would no longer have tracks. She stated, "I thought this was the year that you weeded those kids out." I asked her who "those kids" were. She did not respond. A former principal told me of a parent who would refer to some students as "the time wasters." It was clear to him that the parent was referring to minority students, although she would never publicly admit it.

It is not unusual to find symbols and coded language revealing racial prejudice when the detracking debate becomes public and heated. For example, during the detracking process at another integrated suburban high school in New York, parents of high-track students would appear at school board meetings complaining about "kids whose parents don't care," and "kids who do no work."[6] Likewise, in San Jose, California, parents who opposed detracking referred to it as a means to provide advantage to Latino students at the expense of white students. At a multicultural training event, some parents arrived wearing red, white, and blue while others came dressed in army fatigues.[7]

In a study of three high schools that undertook detracking reforms, researcher Beth Rubin found that the classroom diversity resulting from these efforts was not universally appreciated by parents.[8] She notes that in open forums, parents would complain about resources being diverted from their students to serve high-needs students, and the effects that those students' scores had on the overall public ranking of the schools. One parent described the school as "an urban school in a suburban setting."[9]

The same stereotypes play out in racially homogeneous schools that are diverse in their socioeconomic makeup. During one rural school detracking reform, discussed in a subsequent chapter, social class became the divider. The principal of this New England high school, in which nearly half of the students received free or reduced-priced lunch, received continual pushback from teachers when she began to detrack the school. She was told that she "did not understand the Valley," and that many of the children were incapable of high achievement because their parents were involved in the drug trade. In her reform efforts she repeatedly encountered a classism that reinforced the tracking system of the school.[10]

Coded or overt, stereotypes based on race, class, ethnicity, and/or intelligence creep into the dialogue when the conversation becomes heated. During my interviews, time and again I would hear from school administrators and teachers about how parents who considered themselves to be progressive in their thinking became highly defensive and protective when detracking was discussed. They were proud of sending their children to an integrated school. Integrated middle and high school classrooms, however, were a very different matter.

Sense of Entitlement or System "Ownership"

When I was a teacher in the Lawrence Public Schools, a racially diverse, highly tracked high school, I once had a conversation with a colleague who was also a district resident. She told me "how lucky" the minority students who lived in the district were. Even though they were in low-track classes, they were, in her mind, far better off in her affluent district than in an urban school. She did not understand, she said, "why they were not more grateful and cooperative."

I don't think she truly understood the implications of her remarks. It was clear to me that she believed that she, and people like her, "owned" the district, and that poorer families were interlopers who were out of "their place" and lucky to have found themselves among the white upper middle class. Although all district residents are equally entitled to partake in and govern their own public schools, there is often an underlying belief that some have earned the right, through the payment of a higher tax levy, to have more voice in the governance of those schools. Likewise, there is a belief that the students who are smarter and who work harder should have access to the best teachers and curriculum. In my experience I have found that far too many principals and superintendents have catered to such parents and students and reinforced that belief for fear of the power of the school's "squeakiest wheels."

This is the essence of entitlement and it pervades many school systems. It is the belief that the most active parents and the parents who pay the most in taxes should have their needs and their opinions taken more seriously than the opinions of poorer or less active parents. They often run for the school board or for president of the PTA. If they themselves do not run for office, they are the folks who support candidates who run for the school board and they work to get out the vote. In my decades in education, I have met remarkable and generous board members and PTA leaders who never sought special advantage for their child. But the politics of schools cannot be ignored, and friends and neighbors whisper in ears and speak out at meetings. They make it clear that they want their interests heard. Wealth, parental education, and advocacy often are associated with the highest-achieving students in any given school.

In Woodland Hills, Pennsylvania, which will be discussed in greater detail in the next chapter, a very vocal contingent of white parents who called themselves the Citizens for Quality Education opposed detracking. They were the parents of high achievers, and their argument was that if the district was providing something for *all* children, then it could not possibly be good enough for *their* children. Such parents clearly believed that success was a zero-sum commodity, and that if all students were given access to excellence there would be less for their child, whom they believed to be more deserving.

Jeannie Oakes and Martin Lipton saw this dynamic play out in their study of an integrated high school in a liberal college town located on the East Coast.[11] As the school sought to open the gates to its AP program so that more of its black students would have access, a group of powerful parents immediately began to organize to protect the tracking system by adding what they referred to as a "mid-honors" track for motivated students that they claimed would give them more challenge but still protect the exclusive high-track classes. Although these parents argued that they wished to preserve excellence and "safety," Oakes and Lipton's analysis led to the conclusion that "these expressed objections were other worries as well—that reform threatened their children's privileged position in the school and, with it, their own confidence that success at school would ensure their children's access to economic and political advantages as adults."[12]

As the earliest investigators of tracking noted, much of what schools do with tracking systems is to replicate and sustain the class and income stratification that already exists in society.

Belief in Schools as Meritocracies

Those who support tracking do not wish harm on students consigned to low-track classes. They simply selectively ignore the evidence of the harm that low-track classes do, and mistakenly believe that the slow pace of those classes benefits the students in them. If there are problems with low-track classes, those problems should be addressed and low-track classes should be reformed, they argue. Such parents believe the best solution is to raise the learning expectations in the lower-track class. We know from decades of research, however, that it is not possible to reform low-track classes. The intersection between peer effects, classroom culture, and curriculum pacing works to undo the efforts of even the most skilled teacher.

Defenders of tracking also believe (or purport to believe) that tracking is fair. They think that students who work hard earn their way into high-track classes, and that those who do not, deserve what they get. They also believe that every student has the same opportunity to excel or to choose the high track, and that it is up to them to make the best of it. In Wilmington, Delaware, and Rockford, Illinois, schools made this argument.[13] High tracks were open, they said, if the parent was willing to sign a waiver (thus implying that the parent, not the school, was responsible for making a poor educational choice for the child).

Those who see tracking as meritocratic believe that the "new" systems, commonly referred to as ability grouping or leveling, are inherently fair. The argument heard most often is that these systems, unlike tracking systems of the past in which a student's placement was "fixed," have the benefit of being fluid and flexible. Students, in theory, can move in and out of ability groups.[14] The problem is that there is little evidence that such movement actually occurs. The reality is that ability grouping has proven itself to be a tournament model—once selected into a track or ability group, a student's only likely movement is down, to a lower group or track.[15]

The problem with the meritocratic argument is that it selectively ignores the research that clearly links student performance with factors outside of school, such as the effects of poverty on the development of vocabulary. It ignores how tutoring influences test scores and grades, or the effects that peer pressure have on academic ambition. It ignores research showing that low-track classes, no matter how they are formed or reformed, result in lower student achievement.

Earning access to high-track classes is connected with earning access to the best colleges. For example, in Woodland Hills, the college admissions process reinforced the tracking system. If the gifted and talented program was listed on the student's transcript, parents believed that the child would have an advantage in the admissions process. The same was true of the school's Advanced Placement courses. The weighted grades of AP courses resulted in a higher average. The listing of the course name on the transcript would bring advantage in the college admissions process because it set the student apart and signaled better college preparation.

In his study of "star" public high schools, Paul Attewell describes how some schools limit access to classes like IB and AP in order to enhance the chances of their most competitive students gaining entry to Ivy League colleges.[16] He asserts that schools use sorting and stratification to help some students "stand out from the rest" in the college admissions process. Furthermore, his study suggests that these schools limit access in an attempt to increase average scores on external exams, thus presenting an image of school excellence to further distinguish their AP students.

Ironically, with respect to the college selection process there is no evidence that limited access to AP courses benefits either students or schools. Parents with a competitive mindset, however, perceive that the rarer the school's AP designation, the greater the advantage bestowed on students. Both the weighted grades as well as the course name were seen as bringing earned advantage to students in the admissions process. In addition, the school's teachers, in Attewell's study, were convinced that the College Board wanted prospective AP students to be grouped together and accelerated in order to best prepare them for AP courses.

The tracking system, then, is an extension of the "survival of the fittest" mentality that one person's success is dependent upon another's failure. Advocates of tracking understand this kind of competition to be the natural order of things, and thus fair.

Alliances Among Vested Interests

In his 2001 book, *Legal Rights, Local Wrongs*, Kevin Welner describes how resistant parents aligned themselves with resistant teachers to oppose detracking. Jeannie Oakes and Amy Stuart Wells contend that resistance to detracking is most powerful when there is "an intersection of teachers' beliefs about intelligence and parents' use of status and power."[17] This often manifests itself as an alliance between high-track teachers and the parents of high-track students. In their study of ten detracking schools, the researchers often encountered teachers with a limited, traditional notion of capacity to learn that was grounded in stereotypical beliefs about black, Latino, and Native American children. Teachers would attribute cultural forces to minority students, which they believed limited their intellectual abilities and their motivation to work hard at school. Parents who aligned themselves with these teachers bought into these beliefs. One parent told Oakes and her team that Latino students in the schools were "Mexicans at heart" who had not internalized American values and would drag the class down. When teachers reinforce these worries, and thus legitimize the stereotypes, parents become emboldened and see themselves not only as advocates for their children, but as advocates for teachers who will be victimized when forced to teach low-track students.

It is not unusual for alliances to emerge between parents who oppose detracking and teachers who are resistant to detracking reforms. Often, teachers come to see their assignment to high-track classes as a "perk" earned through seniority. They do not want to give up the privilege. Often there are whisper campaigns in which teachers reinforce the fears of high-track parents that their children's learning will be slowed down by students who are not as bright.

When aligned with such like-minded teachers, parents assure themselves that their cause is just, because, after all, don't the teachers know the students and their needs best? Chapter 7 will provide an example of how just such an alliance functioned in the Woodland Hills School District. Such alliances, to a greater or lesser extent, are quite common, although in the past decade, teachers, armed with research findings and a sense of social justice, appear more inclined to be advocates of detracking than opponents of it. In the stories of detracking that follow, many important examples of teachers as equity advocates will be provided.

The first chapters of this book provided evidence from the literature on the origins of tracking and the problems associated with it. The reader learned how racial and socioeconomic stratification is connected with tracking, regardless of the system that is used to assign students to classes. The reader was also given an overview of the effects of tracking on student achievement, both overall and on subgroups of students. Chapter 5 provided an illustration of one long-term, successful detracking reform. This chapter presented an overview of the normative and political forces that work to inhibit detracking reforms.

What follows are the stories of those who dared to dismantle tracking systems and how they encountered, and in some cases overcame, the forces arrayed against them. From their success, both great and small, those who care about the equitable distribution of learning opportunities for students will have much to learn.

7
Race and Detracking
The Stories of Two Districts

Woodland Hills School District in Pennsylvania and the Stamford Public Schools in Connecticut have much in common. Both were under the watchful eye of the courts and civil rights organizations due to a history of segregation. Woodland Hills was under a court order to desegregate, while Stamford's desegregation was voluntary. Both districts, following school desegregation, engaged in de facto segregation within classrooms by tracking. The courts noted the racial stratification produced by tracking in the classes of Woodland Hills, and a report by the US Commission on Civil Rights made the same observation in Stamford.

Both districts' student bodies were integrated by race and socioeconomic status. The factors that impede detracking, discussed in the last chapter, were very much at play during the districts' reform efforts. In both cases, courageous superintendents saw tracking for what it was and addressed the issue head-on. Despite their convictions, and the support they had from others, the path was hardly smooth.

WOODLAND HILLS SCHOOL DISTRICT

During the 1960s, the Commonwealth of Pennsylvania underwent a process of school-district consolidation.[1] The legislature that crafted district lines clearly did so with race in mind. In the area outside Pittsburgh, lawmakers grouped together several poor districts in which there was a concentration of black students, while at the same time preserving or creating several adjacent districts that were predominantly wealthy and white. Parents in the poorer, predominantly black district, the General Braddock Area School District, saw the redistricting for what it was—an attempt to segregate their children.

In 1971, parents and students of the General Braddock Area School District went to court to file a claim that their school district's formation was a deliberate attempt to discriminate against minority children. In 1974, Judge Gerald Weber found that the consolidation was in fact de jure discrimination, and ordered the commonwealth, state board of education, and county school board to find a remedy, which they were unable to do. In the spring of 1981 the court stepped in and imposed its own remedy, adopting the plan the plaintiffs had proposed. Judge Weber ordered the merger of General Braddock with four other districts whose students were predominantly white and wealthy. Thus, the Woodland Hills School District came into existence.

Creation of the new district was not enough to please the court, however. The district needed a desegregation plan at the elementary level in order to integrate its schools. As the court monitored desegregation efforts as part of the supervisory process, it advised the district that it also needed to address the resegregation of classrooms that resulted from tracking. Following a 1991 court opinion, the district was ordered to remove the vestiges and evidence of prior segregation, and detracking became part of the remedy.

It was in 1991, in the tenth year of court supervision, that superintendent Stanley Herman was hired. He would lead the district for a decade, until Woodland Hills came within reach of unitary status, which meant its release from the supervision of the court. It would be a difficult ten years during which, according to Herman, his "every move was second-guessed by fifteen attorneys."[2] Despite many obstacles, Herman was committed to removing the vestiges of segregation and restoring the district to unitary status. And he knew that a good part of the problem was tracking.

As a former administrator in the Pittsburgh schools, he was familiar with their history of segregation, and the differing expectations associated with tracking. What he found when he got to Woodland Hills did not surprise him. Beginning in the seventh grade, there was a dual curriculum in English. One track was rich in literature and writing. The other was based on grammar instruction and "drill and practice." Although both tracks were ostensibly open to all students, counselors steered students into one or the other by asking questions such as, "Do you want to work hard and to go to college?" Herman believed that black students subtly got the message that the top track was not for them, and about 80 percent opted for the lower track. This stratification between the two tracks continued throughout the high school years.

The differences in track placement could not be explained by students' prior achievement. Although grades and standardized test scores accounted for most of the differences, when these factors were held constant, a white student was 2.3 times more likely to be in a high-track class than a black student. In addition, the long-term negative effects of being in the low track in math or English were dramatic, with low-track placement resulting in students falling further and further behind students with the same scores but who were placed in the high-track pathway.[3]

For Dr. Herman, the order of the court proved to be a blessing. It gave him the cover to do the work he knew needed to be done in a district rife with racial tension. He decided to abolish the two-track system in English and mandate that all students take the high-track curriculum in integrated, detracked classes.

As he began to move the district from a two- to a one-track system in English, he met with strong resistance. Fifty to seventy parents would attend every meeting of the school board to voice their opposition. He told me how students in high-track classes would come to the microphone in tears to say that their college admission chances would be damaged if they were in classes with "those kids," often described to the superintendent as "the kids who don't want to learn."

One of the benefits of being under a court order was that the Commonwealth of Pennsylvania financed 90 percent of the costs of the remedy—thus providing the district with ample resources to do the necessary work. Dr. Herman was able to pay for consulting services as well as supports for students and staff development. Jeannie Oakes, a leading scholar on detracking, and her student, Kevin Welner, thus found themselves in an advisory role at Woodland Hills, providing the district with their expertise and support.

To assist students in the newly heterogeneous classes, Dr. Herman started after-school tutorials in the neighborhoods where they were most needed. About two-thirds of the teaching staff in the tutorial centers were teachers from Woodland Hills. The achievement of minority students improved while the achievement of majority students remained stable. Advanced Placement courses, which had been nearly exclusively white, slowly became more diverse.

In 1995, Dr. Herman opened an Early Childhood Program in the poorest community of the district. Generous funding came from the United Way and the Heinz Foundation, and the University of Pittsburgh carefully documented the achievement of the students who attended. The program was a success. It helped close the achievement gap of students who were two or three years behind their more affluent peers, and that gap remained closed as they progressed through the elementary grades.

Despite this progress, opposition to detracking remained strong.

Although surveys had clearly indicated that low-track classes were not perceived as demanding by students or teachers, and that few teachers wanted to teach them, there was strong resistance to the elimination of the low-track classes. As the classes were blended, teachers tended to "teach to the middle," and some struggled with keeping the high-track expectations alive. The assignment of high-track classes had been a privilege of seniority for teachers, and those who believed that they had earned those classes through putting in the time were loath to give them up. Others had been consigned to the low-track classes and thus did not have experience with the high-track curriculum. The community worried that the AP program would be compromised, despite the absence of evidence that this was the case.

The mathematics department proved to be the most resistant. When Dr. Herman arrived, minority students were stuck in low-level arithmetic-based courses with names such as Applied Math and Practical Math. In 1990, the courts observed that students in such low-level courses were unable to advance to upper-level math courses such as geometry and eventually calculus.[4] They ordered the district to abolish low-level math classes.

Math teachers, however, did not want to give up their plum advanced courses and teach students of varied math ability in the same class. After considering giving all students algebra in grade eight, as recommended by Oakes and Welner and sought by the plaintiffs, the district decided instead to eliminate all low-level math courses and give students the same course offerings, only with different entry points (that is, some students would start algebra in grade eight, while others would take the course in grades nine or ten). By 2000, however, that solution was not implemented to the satisfaction of the courts. Some students were "getting ready to get ready" to take algebra by taking pre-algebra courses not only in middle school, but in high school as well, even as late as grade ten. The courts found that minority students were noticeably absent from higher-level math courses, and overrepresented in basic math. The district continued to work on providing one course of study in math and opening earlier pathways to higher-level math for all students.

In 2003, the district met that obligation to the satisfaction of the courts, and in June it achieved full unitary status. The designation would prove to be a mixed blessing, however, as unitary status meant the end of state funding provided by the court order. For the first time in over a decade, the school district had to pass a budget without the extra funding it had received from the state to achieve unitary status.

Attorney Ed Feinstein, who represented the plaintiffs, expressed his concern to a reporter with the local newspaper.[5] Without the pressure of the court and the funding that came along with it, would the district backslide and return to old practices? When the budget cuts came, which students would be most impacted?

The math labs, which provided one-on-one math help in the school, and in the community, were slated for elimination. Curriculum coordinators, who were key players in the implementation of the detracked curriculum, were reduced in number. The instructional coaches who helped teachers change their practices as the classes became more heterogeneous were cut.

Dr. Herman had retired in 2001, and slowly his team left the district. Gradually there were calls in the district to do something for the "bright kids." Honors English and math classes were restored. There are now courses called Applied English and Applied Math as well as sections of courses in both math and English that isolate special education students. Mr. Feinstein's worries were apparently well founded.[6]

In Woodland Hills in 2012, there was a gifted program and three courses at the Advanced Placement level in math—Calculus-AB, Calculus-BC, and Statistics. Woodland Hills has become a majority-minority district. The closing of the achievement gap in English, of which Dr. Herman was so proud, has not been maintained. The district's achievement gap across subgroups speaks for itself (see table 7.1).[7]

Table 7.1
Achievement Results (2012) by Subgroup,
Woodland Hills School District

	# TESTED MATH	% ADV. MATH	% PROF. MATH	% BASIC MATH	% BELOW BASIC
White	576	48.1	29.9	13.0	9.0
Black	1202	20.9	33.1	23.3	22.7
Hispanic	25	24.0	44.0	4.0	28.0
Asian	16	50.0	31.3	18.8	0.0

	# TESTED ENGLISH	% ADV. ENGLISH	% PROF. ENGLISH	% BASIC ENGLISH	% BELOW BASIC
White	576	34.9	38.9	15.6	10.6
Black	1201	13.6	32.1	24.3	30.0
Hispanic	25	20.0	24.0	36.0	20.0
Asian	16	18.8	62.5	18.8	0.0

It is difficult to ascertain whether the return to tracking was the result of the retirement of the administrators who had championed the detracking reform, or the fact that detracking was never fully embraced by the community and staff. (Funding was also noted as an issue. When the state funds ran out, the programs that sustained detracking were quickly put on the chopping block.)

From my own experience and from what the research on detracking shows, I would conclude that it was a bit of both. Because the order came from the courts, there was no time to lay the normative groundwork for the change. There were few if any successful models of detracked secondary schools, and while there was ample professional development, it was taking place at the same time that detracking was happening. When the leadership that sustained it left, there was not a critical mass to support it. It was easy to go back to the status quo, and the lack of funding became the excuse, but of course not the real reason. Certainly, detracking could have been sustained without the additional funding by reallocating resources, obtaining grants, or even continuing with fewer supports.

As the proportion of minority students grew to be the majority, the district appears to have resorted to what so many districts in similar circumstances do—it sought to create a school within a school that caters primarily to high-achieving students in hopes of staving off white flight. The promise of a school that prepared all students equally for college and career was lost.

STAMFORD PUBLIC SCHOOLS

School superintendent Josh Starr will tell you that the reduction of tracking in the Stamford, Connecticut, schools is one of the accomplishments of which he is most proud.[8] School equity advocate and parent activist Wendy Lecker will tell you that she is proud, too, but that there is more work to be done. The reduction in tracking in the middle schools of Stamford is a story of a reform accomplished in the face of tremendous political opposition.

The Stamford Public Schools enroll fifteen thousand students. There are twenty schools—some are neighborhood schools while others are magnet schools. Twenty-one percent of the district's students are African American, 7 percent are Asian American, 32 percent are Latino, and 40 percent are white. Fifty-four percent of all students are considered disadvantaged, as determined by one or more of the following factors—free or reduced-priced lunch status, ELL status, and residence in low-income housing.

Like Woodland Hills in Pennsylvania, the history of tracking in Stamford is intertwined with a history of school segregation. In 1971, Stamford Public Schools began a voluntary desegregation policy—no school could be more than 10 percent over or under the district percentage of any ethnic group. The Stamford Board of Education used three strategies to integrate district schools—the construction of new schools in "neutral" areas; busing (primarily of black and Latino students to predominantly white schools); and magnet schools.

Although the school sites were desegregated, as was the case in Woodland Hills, the classrooms at the middle and high school level had been resegregated via tracking. Some elementary schools began "ability grouping" in grade three or even earlier. The middle schools had three to five ability tracks. In 1976, as noted in an earlier chapter, the Connecticut Advisory Committee to the US Commission on Civil Rights initiated a review of the status of Stamford's progress with desegregation, and expressed concern that middle and high-school ability grouping was resegregating classrooms, with high-track students being predominantly white, and low-track students being predominantly black or Latino. The report notes that although some parents and students favored ability grouping, others spoke out against the practice at the middle and high school level. For example, a strong statement in favor of detracking, made by Charles Ukkerd, the African American director of a local community center and a parent, was recorded in the report. The conclusion of the commission was clear—it found that "ability grouping as it now operates tends to re-segregate the school system and reinforce feelings of inadequacy in minority students in the middle and high schools," and it went on to recommend that ability grouping be abolished whenever feasible, and that the place to start was at the middle school level.[9]

However, nearly thirty years after the report, when Dr. Starr arrived in 2005 as superintendent, it appeared that no progress on that recommendation had been made. The tracking system of the district was essentially as it had been described in 1976. Josh Starr understood the importance of integrating classrooms and decided that detracking Stamford's rigidly tracked schools would be "his signature work." As he began quiet conversations on detracking, he found that his advisers were as split as the schools' demographics—about 50 percent told him to take it on as an issue and the other 50 percent said it would be his undoing and to let it go. The more he looked at the data, the more he knew that pursuing detracking reform was the right thing to do.

The gap in the proficiency rates between the students in the upper and lower tracks was dramatic, and because the tracks were racially stratified, the achievement gap was wide. Dr. Starr knew the research. The question for him was not *whether* the schools should be detracked, but how the reform should be implemented. He realized that he would need to build support for the initiative over time. For three years, he quietly garnered support through one-on-one and small-group conversations with staff, parents, and community members. He did not directly address the issue of tracking. Instead, he talked about the practices of heterogeneous and homogeneous student grouping and how they affected student learning.

Starr characterized the Stamford schools as being like "the wild west" when he arrived—no curricular structures, with everyone doing their own thing. He would jokingly remark that there were twenty schools with eighty different ways of doing business. He was not far off the mark. A Phi Delta Kappan elementary literacy survey found that there were 153 reading programs among the twelve elementary schools in the district.[10] It made sense to Starr, therefore, to nest his tracking reform within the context of a larger reform of the district's middle schools. As he observed during my interview with him, "I cannot take something away without providing a better product." When I asked him to identify the "something" that would be taken away, he defined it as the "privilege" associated with access to high-track classes.

Indeed, a sense of privilege, and the stratification it supported, was evident in the district. As I searched for written materials to support the interviews that form the foundation of this chapter, I found the following on the blog of a local newspaper in January of 2011, even after tracking had been reduced. It was written in response to an inquiry regarding the quality of the schools.

> In fact, [tracking] is the single most important aspect you should focus to ensure your child(ren) receive the best education. Students from the better neighborhoods in the city are almost automatically placed in the highest levels while the students from the poorer neighborhoods are concentrated in the lower levels. If you make sure your kids are included in the upper levels in each grade (once they are placed in such level, they will be maintained there in the subsequent years) then you have little to worry about . . . While the schools as a whole may not be showing desirable achievement levels, keep in mind that there is a strong schism between overachieving students and the underachieving ones, with not much left in the middle. It's almost as if two different schools are meshed together in one building. Or to put it another way and depending on the point of view, the public schools' scores are either "lifted" by the better students or "dragged down" by the less serious ones. But, it's important to mention that the two groups don't necessarily mix.[11]

Clearly there was and still is a tacit understanding held by some residents that two systems had been built in the district—one that focused resources serving primarily white and Asian American upper-middle-class students and another serving primarily African American and Latino students who, for the most part, were poor. As long as parents from the "better" neighborhood got their children placed in the high-track classes, those children would receive a good education apart from the rest.

Josh Starr was not alone in his fight for social justice and equal educational opportunity. Cindy Grafstein is a longtime advocate for students, serving in leadership roles in the parent organizations of the Stamford Public Schools at every level. She also recognized how tracking created a dual system, and she disliked its effects on Stamford's students and families. She told me that nearly every white parent would try to get their children in the high track, called the "zero group." If that could not be achieved, then the "one group," which was also composed of predominantly white students, was the second option. There appeared to be a tremendous "fear factor" among parents, and that caused a level of anxiety that was not healthy for parents or for students.

There was one middle school, a magnet school called Scofield, with no tracking at all. Cindy Grafstein's son attended Scofield, and she was delighted with the education that he received. The classes were mixed in both race and achievement, with frequent regrouping of students so that kids got to know all of their classmates rather than being assigned to the same group year after year. According to Grafstein, "There was no anxiety at all and if there were any regrouping based on academics, no one student or parent knew it."[12] But Scofield was the exception in a highly tracked and stratified system.

Figure 7.1 shows just how stratified the middle school tracks were two years after Josh Starr's arrival.[13] Although only 40 percent of all students in the district were white, nearly 79 percent of the honors track was white. As overrepresented as white students were in the honors track, they were underrepresented in the three lowest tracks. Conversely, although 53 percent of the district's students were black or Latino, only 11 percent of the honors track was black or Latino. In the three lowest tracks, however, about 73 percent of the students were black or Latino.

In order to build support for his detracking initiative, Josh Starr formed a think tank, which evolved into the Middle School Transformation Committee, to review data and create a rigorous curriculum for all students. At the same time, the committee was charged with reviewing the organizational structure of the middle school and, based on research, recommending the strategies and structures that would achieve the goal of providing challenging learning opportunities for all of Stamford's children. To help fund the transformation initiative, Starr secured a grant from the General Electric Foundation, which initially awarded the schools $15.3 million of a grant that would eventually total a very generous $27 million. Detracking became an integral part of a greater reform effort that addressed curriculum, professional development, and research-based practices.

In order to lay the groundwork for the detracking reform, Starr worked on informing the committee and the community at large. He began by putting the data out regarding the tracking gap and the achievement gap. He described the kind of instruction that he wanted to see in the middle school classrooms. At the same time, he created a relationship and alliance with the local NAACP and

Figure 7.1
Distribution of Ethnic Groups Across Tracks, Stamford Public Schools

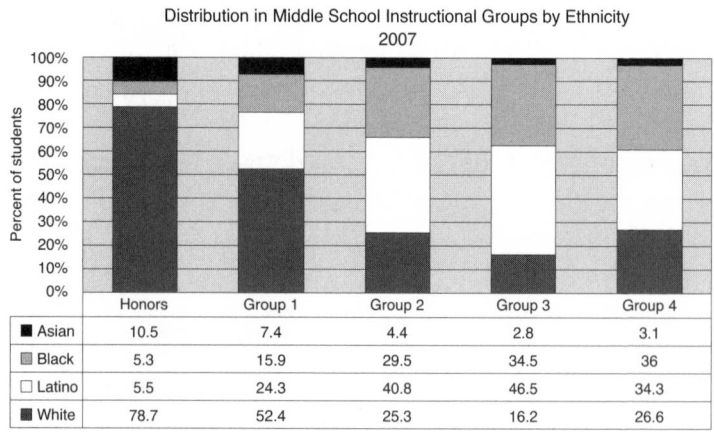

Distribution in Middle School Instructional Groups by Ethnicity 2007

	Honors	Group 1	Group 2	Group 3	Group 4
■ Asian	10.5	7.4	4.4	2.8	3.1
▨ Black	5.3	15.9	29.5	34.5	36
☐ Latino	5.5	24.3	40.8	46.5	34.3
■ White	78.7	52.4	25.3	16.2	26.6

Latino community and began to talk openly about race, encouraging difficult conversations within the boundaries of respect and community norms.

The Middle School Transformation Committee attracted serious and committed school and community members. PT Council activists Wendy Lecker and Cindy Grafstein's service on the transformation committee reinforced for them what they already suspected about tracking. A parent of three children in the Stamford Schools, and having served as staff attorney for the Campaign for Fiscal Equity in New York, Lecker had a deep commitment to social justice. Although her oldest daughter was in the desirable "zero," or top academic group, she was uneasy with the middle school's tracking system. She did not believe that her daughter was as challenged as she should have been, or even as challenged as she had been in her heterogeneously grouped elementary school. She wondered why honors existed at all. What concerned her more, however, was that she was in a class that was almost all white, even though more than half of the students in the district were students of color.

Cindy Grafstein saw how different her son's experience in the detracked Scofield Magnet School was compared with her daughter's experience in one of the district's tracked middle schools. When her daughter admitted to being happy that the honors kids were grouped apart from everyone else, Grafstein became dismayed and angry. "It made me realize that the kids at Scofield were in a much healthier environment than my daughter was," Grafstein told me. "I basically had to deprogram my daughter from that train of thought. I saw my son, who attended Scofield, work on a complicated exhibition project next to a girl who was working on a not-so-complicated project, but neither of them knew of the other's level of ability—to them they were both just working on their project. At my daughter's middle school, only the 'smart' kids were assigned to do History Day and everyone knew it. There was no expectation at all, by the teachers or the students, that any student but the ones in the top group could do a research project. That was shocking to me."

Lecker and Grafstein voraciously read all of the research they could find on tracking and shared it widely, coming to the conclusion that detracking would bring a better, more equitable educational experience to Stamford's schools. According to Lecker, "The research confirmed what I witnessed as a parent in a heterogeneously grouped elementary school and a homogeneously grouped middle school. The heterogeneous grouping did not harm the 'high performing' children academically, whereas homogeneous grouping harmed children who were placed in the lower group. Those children were foreclosed from learning opportunities in middle school (like foreign languages) and they were foreclosed from learning opportunities throughout high school, such as four years of science and math, and AP classes. Moreover, the segregation resulting from homogeneous grouping in middle school harmed all children by depriving them of the opportunity of learning together and from each other."

Cindy Grafstein's view was informed by her own observations regarding the importance of the middle school experience in the emotional growth of the student. "Putting aside all of the research, pro and con, the issue is simple—if a middle school student is happy, content, and comfortable, then he/she will want to learn. I truly believe that middle school is almost as much about social and emotional development as it is about academic development. I just saw happier kids in general at Scofield—kids that didn't have any of the baggage that goes along with ability grouping. It was unbelievable to me that we were basically teaching our kids prejudice in such an insidious way via tracking."

Both Lecker and Grafstein believe that if given the chance, the committee would have recommended that all of the district's middle schools be structured like Scofield. Ironically, parents who believed in tracking were now competing for a spot for their child in the detracked magnet. In the end, however, the total elimination of tracking was not seen as politically feasible.

The Middle School Transformation Committee made a series of recommendations that included the following:

- Development of a rigorous curriculum that would be taught in all middle schools

- Extensive professional development for all teachers

- Revision of track-placement guidelines to ensure that students were not placed in the same track across the curriculum

- Elimination of the lower tracks, resulting in a two-track system for the middle school—honors and college prep

The report and its recommendations received the support of the local newspaper, the *Stamford Advocate*, which quoted from the report of the Connecticut Advisory Committee to the US Commission on Civil Rights and opined that "rigid tracking dooms those stuck in low levels to the ghetto of low expectations."[14] The committee was proud of its efforts and looked forward to truly transforming the middle schools of Stamford into more equitable and excellent schools.

The General Electric Foundation supported the committee's work, and the funding it supplied gave Josh Starr the resources required to build the professional development systems and rich curricula that were needed to do the reform right. He continued to lay out the data and coupled it with the question, "Why do we allow some kids to suffer in the low-track classes?" Many teachers, especially young teachers, were on board with detracking. They worked together to learn how to differentiate instruction and to provide the needed support to students.

Detracking and middle school reform were implemented during the 2009–10 school year. State test scores went up for all subgroups, with accelerated growth for black and Latino students. A survey of parents, students, and teachers showed positive reactions to the reform. *Flexible grouping* (the term that Starr used to describe the decoupling of tracking in math and English) with broader track-placement criteria, replaced the rigid tracking system so that students could be in honors for one class but in college prep for another. The percentage of black or Latino students in the honors math track increased from 11 percent to 30 percent—a dramatic shift in the proportion of student groups in the highest track.

Teachers began to ask, "Why are we still grouping at all?" Wendy Lecker and Cindy Grafstein asked, "Why are we not giving the honors curriculum to all students?" The hope was to further reduce tracking in the district, eliminating low-track classes by 2014.

As detracking was implemented, however, there was growing opposition among some parents. The opposition became well organized and adopted the name "Stamford's Residents for Excellence in Education." More than three hundred Stamford parents signed a petition opposing detracking. Some parents threatened "white flight" either by moving out of the district or by sending their children to private schools.[15] They argued that tracking should not be fixed and should be made more flexible, but that grouping students into multiple levels should not be eliminated. Two tracks, they contended, were not enough. They were upfront in expressing their belief that the diversity of the community demanded multiple ability groups in English language arts and math because there was, in their opinion, too much diversity to be accommodated in a two-tier system.[16] There was also the underlying fear that eventually the two tracks would become one. They claimed they rejected tracking but supported ability grouping, adopting a distinction between the two that few make. The members of Stamford's Residents for Excellence in Education became both politically active and motivated and began to seek like-minded candidates who would run in the next school board election.

Wendy Lecker, for whom all of the reforms made sense, was astounded by the tone of the debate. As she became a vocal supporter of detracking, she was accused of dividing the community and "playing to race." She recounted being told to "stick to bake sales," and that she was doing something "dangerous" by making herself part of a "radical fringe."

Stamford Board of Education member and former board president Jackie Heftman was also surprised and appalled by the tone of the debate.[17] Josh Starr had been hired with the mission of closing the achievement gap. According to Heftman, the board understood that there was something very wrong with tracking, but because it had been such a traditional part of the school culture, it had never been truly questioned.

During the beginning of his superintendency, Heftman noted, Josh Starr had strong support, but when he introduced detracking, "all hell broke loose"—it appeared as though some residents developed "a hate on for Josh." He held positions on race and tracking that some of his early supporters had never expected.

At first the opposition was neither strong nor strident, but then the two political parties jumped into the fray. In Stamford, school board candidates run on either the Democrat or Republican ticket. The two party chairs nominate forty committee members who then screen potential candidates. Because of this system, the party chairs, through the nominating process, wield tremendous influence with respect to which candidates get to run for the school board.

The longtime chairperson of Stamford's Democratic City Committee, Ellen Camhi, served as Stamford Board of Education president when the civil rights report that called for a reduction in tracking was first issued. Her son, Keith Camhi, who was a leader of Stamford Residents for Excellence in Education, was opposed to the two-group system. The Republican chairperson was opposed to detracking as well. A candidate who supported the reform was highly unlikely to get on the ticket of either party. Opposition to detracking became a litmus test.

Jackie Heftman and other interviewees believe that if the party chairs had not gotten involved, there would have been far less opposition to the reform. Everything changed when the issue became politicized. In the next election, two board members who opposed detracking were elected. The following year brought another two. The board became divided in its support for the reform and for Josh Starr. Stamford Residents for Excellence in Education supported those candidates who opposed detracking, claiming that a system with "multiple, flexible groups" was better than the present two-level system. The only real "flexibility" that was supported, however, was that students could be in different tracks for different subjects. It became a battle of semantics.

Starr held his ground despite the opposition. In an opinion piece on the topic, he stated, "Some may think we have a choice about eliminating tracking. I do not. If we want to live up to the ideals of social justice and equity long espoused by our community, we must ensure that each and every one of our children has access to a curriculum based on high standards that prepares them to graduate ready for higher education and success in the 21st century."[18] For Josh Starr, the reduction in tracking became, as he told me when I interviewed him, "the hill that I was willing to die on."

As the board changed from the one that selected Starr to one in which the new members opposed him, the dispute became more contentious. Board members began asking trivial questions and micromanaging the running of the schools. At public meetings, Starr reported that his statements were often twisted. Any opportunity to undermine the reform effort was seized upon by those opposed to the reform.

Over time, every meeting of the board became highly politicized and polarized. Starr held to his optimistic view that most parents (90 percent) are reasonable and that you cannot argue with the data. The achievement gap was closing, and student scores were on the rise. Finally, at one meeting in the fall of 2010, he was challenged by a board member to make his best argument for detracking.

Starr relished the challenge and made a two-and-a-half-hour presentation on the history of tracking and racial stratification since the 1970s. He was not alone in voicing his support. Faculty members who attended the meeting also spoke out in favor of the reform and the reduction in tracking.

Teachers spoke about the inequities of tracking not only from the standpoint of their teaching, but also from their experiences as students in the Stamford school system. A seventh-grade language arts teacher from the Turn of River Middle School supported detracked classes and spoke of the damage done to her own classmates' futures because of the tracking system that was in place when she attended Stamford Schools. A teacher of eighth-grade social studies spoke of the de facto segregation in eighth-grade classes where tracking still existed and how the low track did not serve students well. Wendy Lecker told a local reporter that Starr's presentation "made me proud to say I live in Stamford."[19]

Support for the reform came from groups outside the school system as well. The president of the local NAACP threatened legal action if the board backpedaled and reinstated tracking.[20] Josh Starr solicited and received a letter of support from the Connecticut commissioner of education, which referenced the state board of education's resolution against tracking; he also secured a statement of support from the GE Foundation that made it clear that the grant would not be continued if the district restored middle school tracking. In February of 2011, Bob Corcoran, the GE Foundation president, told the members of the school board's curriculum committee that funding was dependent on the district's commitment to detracking and that the foundation would take back the funding "in a heartbeat" if the district returned to its tracking practices in any form.[21] In the end, the board of education decided to stay the course, but still the opposition continued.

When he spoke with me, over a year after those contentious meetings, Josh Starr, now the superintendent of Montgomery County,

Maryland, said that every superintendent has to decide whether he or she is Moses or Joshua. He said the question you must ask yourself is, "Will you lead them out and force through the change, or do you want to manage it?" He decided that he needed to be a Moses, and that it was now time to leave. Starr knew that he had become a lightning rod, and while he had shepherded detracking through grade seven, it was now time for someone else to continue its implementation. He would leave that to his supporter and assistant, then deputy, now superintendent, Winnie Hamilton.

For the time being the two-tier system in the middle school is in place, and level-placement criteria are still a flashpoint for discussion. At this point, Starr believes that the work needs to be carried forward by the principals. "I had to blow it up, but the leadership should not come from central. It is now all about the principalship." There are still those who want to dial the reform back. They continue to insist that a multitiered ability–group system is not tracking, and that the diversity of the district requires multiple levels for instruction. It will be up to Winnie Hamilton, her principals, and other like-minded citizens and educators to bring the reform forward.

LESSONS LEARNED

Researcher Paul George talks about how difficult it is to detrack the bimodal school.[22] In both cases described in this chapter, tracking was an extension of former segregation practices. Although many parents may have believed in the efficacy of tracking as a way to promote student learning, it was clear that in both districts it resulted in stark differences in educational opportunities for students, as well as racially identifiable classes. The stratification among the classes could not have been missed. Parents in Woodland Hills believed that tracking was fair because students in Woodland Hills could in theory choose their tracks. Parents in Stamford believed that tracking was fair because of the elaborate track-placement criteria, which allowed those who favored tracking to argue that it was objective and a meritocracy. Ironically, the principals of Stamford were (and still are) constantly under pressure from white parents to place their child in the high-track class. Clearly, it was tacitly understood by savvy parents that the high track brought advantage regardless of student "ability" or merit.

In both districts, codes were used to mask racial prejudice and stereotypes, but nevertheless it was obvious to those who were fighting the battle to detrack that the issue of heterogeneous grouping was more than an instructional issue. Wendy Lecker was accused of "playing to race," and in both cases, "white flight" was a threat used to try to thwart detracking. The district took pride in having schools that were desegregated, but, in the minds of many, desegregation should not extend to the classroom. One interviewee, who wished to remain anonymous, spoke to me about how many of her neighbors had unfounded fears of the integrated lunchroom and of integrated classrooms. This conflict between liberal values and the enactment of liberal policies is not uncommon. What occurred in Stamford recalls the conversation I had with a colleague, recounted earlier, who believed that the minority students who went to school in the affluent, highly tracked district in which we taught should consider themselves "lucky" to be there. The parent of the child of color from a low-SES home is not viewed as having ownership of the system in the same way as the parent who pays higher taxes. There exists an unspoken belief that the paying of higher taxes should result in a better education for kids from affluent homes—and that those less fortunate are "lucky" to be in the school district in the first place.

It is difficult to know if detracking would have even been considered in Woodland Hills had it not been for the involvement of the courts. Unlike Stamford, Woodland Hills was a district that was forced to desegregate. Stanley Herman had the mandate from the courts to support his detracking reform—and it was from that mandate that detracking began. That was both an advantage and a disadvantage. It was an advantage in that the decision to detrack was not subject to debate—the reform was mandated by the court. The fact that the reform was imposed, however, prevented the district from doing the necessary groundwork and building support within the faculty and community. Surely, for some teachers and parents, the court's intervention was seen as a punishment, which further fueled resentment.

Detracking in Woodland Hills was also viewed as a reform that was highly dependent on funding from outside the district. When that funding was taken away, the reduction in resources served as an easy excuse to abandon the reform. Woodland Hills had the additional disadvantage of a lack of support for detracking among the faculty. Elitism within the ranks resulted in entrenched support for the track structure, creating a powerful source of opposition to reform that eventually seized the opportunity to retrack.

In the case of Stamford, the push for detracking came not from the outside, but from Josh Starr and those who recognized the inequities of the system. There was no external mandate and so the rationale had to be carefully built upon the research regarding detracking. As we know from chapter 3, however, there are some studies that claim high-track advantage due to the curricula of high-track classes and the coupling of highly skilled teachers and honors classes. The parents of many high-track students in Stamford would claim that their children were advantaged by the system, and they did not want to risk losing that advantage. Those studies that supported their position would become their ammunition. They readily seized upon the term *flexible grouping*, asserting that the system accommodated all learners and that instead of dismantling it, reforms should be aimed at making it more fair. They never acknowledged how the advantages of a more affluent home, access to out-of-school enrichment, or the cumulative effects of tracking might make the selection system naturally unfair and incapable of being reformed.

Although there were no alliances between high-track parents and teachers (indeed, the middle school teachers were supportive of the effort) in Stamford, there were alliances between parents and the local political system. The vested interest in tracking of some local politicians influenced who was chosen to run for the school board. The vocal opposition of some parents gave politically ambitious members of the community a platform on which to run. Tracking, which is a nuanced and complex issue, can seem to make sense on the surface. Not unlike many educational issues, there is a popular appeal that can attract votes in an election in which the average voter has neither the time nor the interest to deeply explore the issue.

Both superintendents showed extraordinary courage and both told me that they would fight the battle again if given the chance. If Dr. Stanley had stayed longer in Woodland Hills and had the time to build greater support, the reform may have continued. It was understandable, though, that he would be ready for a new challenge after a decade of doing the difficult and important work of bringing the district to unitary status.

As for Josh Starr, he did what he set out to accomplish, which was to reduce tracking, and by taking on the task of dismantling a very elaborate and regressive tracking system, he put himself in a position where he would be limiting his effectiveness going forward. Every issue was becoming a battle. By the time he left he had a bare majority of support on the board. Whether it would have been feasible to institute the Scofield Magnet School model in all of the middle schools, as many committee members wanted, remains an open question. The courageous parents, school board members, faculty, and community members who remain in the district can only hope that the gains will be preserved, and in time there will again be leaders who will further detrack the schools.

8

Tracking and Leadership

In *Detracking for Excellence and Equity*, Delia Garrity and I identified the "three P's" that sustain tracking—prejudice, prestige, and power.[1] From what I have learned from the interviews and research that I have conducted for this book, I now believe that privilege is a far more potent force to be reckoned with than prestige when it comes to maintaining tracking. Privilege ("I do more, I pay more, my child is gifted, therefore I am entitled to . . .") manifests itself in all aspects of public schooling, especially in suburban schools. It is deeply enmeshed in both prejudice and power.

Clearly, the three P's were a part of the stories of Woodland Hills and Stamford and, to a lesser extent, Rockville Centre. The previous two chapters provided anecdotes about how all three work together to undermine, and in some cases overpower, detracking reforms. When all three converge, as they did in the case of Woodland Hills, the reform can be as short-lived as the tenure of the leader who proposes it.

This chapter will focus on three high schools where educators made a deliberate decision to detrack, knowing full well that they would encounter, to some degree, resistance grounded in prejudice, power, and privilege. They were not pressured to detrack by the courts or commissions. They detracked because they were motivated by a sense of social justice and guided by the belief that all students benefit when they are educated together, equitably. In all three cases, school leaders made a conscious decision to take on the three P's, despite the furor that they knew would arise. This chapter will discuss the successful strategies they used and give insight into why school leaders move forward, with eyes wide open, right into the storm they know they will encounter. More importantly, this chapter will tell how they moved through the storm and stayed on course to achieve their goals.

NEW ENGLAND COUNTRY SCHOOL: PREJUDICE AND LOW EXPECTATIONS

"New England Country School" is a pseudonym for a grades 7–12 school in a rural area of New England. Nearly all the students are white and less than 70 percent go on to college. The school enrolls fewer than five hundred students, with a little more than one-third receiving free or reduced-price lunch.

It is a school with generous funding, thanks to an equitable state formula, yet it struggles to keep its enrollment at the levels needed to offer its programs. Student test results are slightly below the state average.

With fewer than seventy students per grade level, it makes little sense to track students, and yet traditionally New England Country School has done so in math for grades seven through twelve and in the upper grade levels of the high school in English, social studies, and science. The belief that supported the multiple levels was that students should not be made to do school work that they resisted—if they wanted an easier path they should be allowed to take it. That mindset changed when Miriam Reynolds was hired as principal.[2]

Reynolds began her career in what she referred to as a "big picture school" that believed in multiple pathways to graduation, which were called "academies." She deeply believed at the time that if students followed their interests, and that if schoolwork was grounded in real-world experiences, learning would be enhanced. She became a trainer and a spokesperson for the program. After a few years, however, she began to question whether the academy format was serving the needs of all students, especially those who chose the less rigorous pathways.

Reynolds noticed how the division of students based on interest resulted in very different educational experiences for students. She was especially troubled by what she observed regarding the Career Academy, which had a vocational thrust. The students in it did little academic work. The students who had a strong academic interest gravitated to the more academic programs, and they did well, while the students in Career Academy floundered.

Although she had been seriously vested in multiple-pathway education, Miriam could not ignore the evidence. She began to believe that all students deserved access to a more challenging curriculum in heterogeneous classes, and she began to question tracking in any of its forms, including student choice systems.

Reynolds found a board of education and a superintendent who were interested in making sure that all students were academically challenged at New England Country. That was the mission for which she was hired. They saw the gaps between middle-class and poor students in the school, and like Reynolds, they were compelled for the sake of social justice to see them close. In addition to an SES gap, there was a gender gap, with boys comprising 80 percent of the population of low-track classes. As Reynolds noted, the low-track classes had a culture of their own and it was not good.

And so she developed a multiyear plan to detrack the school, gradually reducing tracks so that by 2014–15, there would be only two tracks in math, and one course of studies with heterogeneous grouping in all other subjects, from grades seven through twelve. The school is well on its way. It has reduced tracking in math and is slowly reducing tracks in other subject areas. The 2013 school year began with no tracking in English in grades nine through eleven.

However, despite the support from central administration, the road has not been easy. As was the case of all of the schools discussed previously, there has been resistance.

Oddly, the resistance to detracking did not come from parents or from the community. The resistance came from the school faculty. A prejudice existed that held tracking in place in this quaint rural school where there was no racial diversity. The prejudice that can exist in single-race schools in some ways can be more insidious than in racially mixed schools. Teachers, who generally see themselves as socially progressive, tend to mask racial prejudice in presenting themselves as protectors of the gifted child or the "serious" student and his or her rights. In single-race schools, classism and intellectual prejudice are more out in the open. When race is not involved, intellectual prejudice can appear to be socially acceptable.

When detracking first began, the teachers would say that Miriam Reynolds did not understand "the Hillside"—the region where the poorer students lived. There was a stereotype that the parents of the students who lived in the hills did not care about education and made a living through illegal means. The belief was that kids "from the boonies" had no desire to go to college and would not be successful even if they did. They would only drag the class down if they were in with the students who wanted to learn and pursue a college education. Those were the students that the school must save.

The idea that in order for children to learn they must be grouped with students of similar ability and aspirations is based on the misconception that teachers must always teach to the middle, and therefore that heterogeneity in the classroom will leave some students behind and slow others down. The other misconception that fuels intellectual prejudice is that we can measure intelligence and determine suitable life paths by that measurement, and that if we do not prepare students for the appropriate path, we are simply setting them up for failure. This of course was the thinking at the turn of the twentieth century when tracking was introduced, and it was part of the culture of New England Country when Miriam Reynolds first arrived.

An anecdote from my own experience is relevant here. A few years ago a group of teachers and administrators from a high school similar to mine came to learn more about our open-enrollment IB classes. During part of the day, the visiting teachers met with South Side faculty and administration. The Advanced Placement history teacher from the visiting school began wondering aloud whether open enrollment could work in her class. She told the group that she suspected it would not, because lower-achieving students simply had "nothing to offer the class." A shocked silence fell upon the room. The teacher who made the remark was not fazed by the reaction. I filled the silence by remarking that our school philosophy was that our classes existed to serve students, not the other way around.

Intellectual prejudice is not uncommon, and it took a while for the teachers of New England Country to come to terms with it. They had to internalize that a student who does not read or write as well as another, or who comes from a home with fewer academic resources, can still provide rich insights during class discussions. They had to learn that there are ways to make literature more accessible to struggling readers and that support, provided by them, plays a key role in the process. Reynolds instituted a program of professional development to show teachers that support classes could be more than centers for homework help—they could be effective ways to further instruction.

Many of us who were educated in tracked schools are comfortable with our intellectual prejudices and thus do not question whether grouping practices are socially just and, more importantly, effective. And so we make assumptions. We assume that curriculum in the heterogeneous classroom will be, out of necessity, watered down and that students with weaker skills will be frustrated and act out with bad behavior. One only need compare the behavior of students in a heterogeneous class with a low-track class to quickly dispel that myth. However, intellectual prejudice seeks to protect the high-track student from the possibility of disruptive behavior, because intellectual prejudice leads one to believe that high-track students are the jewels of the school and the reason that schools were designed.

Miriam Reynolds understood that the intellectual prejudices and misconceptions she encountered at New England Country could not be dismissed or ignored. She understood that she was changing the way her teachers viewed their students, and that in some cases, she was challenging decades of instructional practice. The teachers at New England Country were good people who believed that they were socially just. No one had ever challenged their beliefs, and so they had not experienced cognitive dissonance.

And so Reynolds moved forward with patience and persistence. She involved as many voices as she could in the process without sacrificing her principles. There were times when she had to firmly state her "nonnegotiables" to those who remained committed to tracking. She always supported teachers along the way. She gave them time to visit detracked schools, ample professional development, and most importantly, she did not overwhelm them with other initiatives.

Slowly, tracking was reduced, beliefs and practices changed, and the school is on its way to being transformed. Miriam Reynolds recognized the barriers and worked in the space where they existed, in the minds of the faculty. She told me that for her, the work was all about social justice. That was what motivated her years earlier to join the multiple-pathways movement, and it was what led her to believe that that program was not providing education equal in rigor to all.

It is easier to see the stratification that tracking causes in a mixed-race school. I used to be able to walk the halls of the high school where I taught and guess the track just by looking in the doorway and observing the race and ethnicity of the students in the class. It is far more difficult to see the inequities when socioeconomic class is the factor that distinguishes the different tracks. Miriam Reynolds was sensitive to the injustice of poverty, and she helped her teachers see what they had not seen before.

RACE AND POWER AT SULLINS HIGH SCHOOL

Sullins High is the lone high school of Baywater Schools, a well-resourced district just outside a major city in the northeastern United States.[3] Some of Sullins High's fifteen hundred students come from homes that are wealthy, primarily located in an area called Lyons Bay. Other students come from households where parents are among the working poor or receive government assistance. These homes are located in the center of a small village that is part of the district. About 25 percent of all students receive free or reduced-priced lunch, and nearly one-third of all students are black or Latino. Although the overall test scores of the school are not bad, a substantial performance gap exists between the school's white and black students. The school struggles to make AYP (the federal No Child Left Behind [NCLP] measure of "adequate yearly progress") for all graduation subgroups, and the outcomes are especially weak for special education students.

This was the school that Thomas Patel found when he arrived as principal. For the previous several years, he was an assistant principal at a neighboring high school not that far from Sullins. It was a non-diverse, affluent school that had reduced tracking while he was there. Patel saw firsthand the growth in student achievement that resulted from detracking in his former high school.

As in the case of Miriam Reynolds, Patel was hired with a specific purpose. The superintendent who hired him wanted the district detracked and the achievement gaps to close. Superintendent Sol Simons was certain that tracking was one of the primary reasons the district's minority students were not succeeding as they should.

He was ready to take on the challenge at the high school level, and he hired Dr. Patel to do the job.

When Patel arrived, he immediately saw the problem. He described the education system in place at the school as "segregation" and "almost criminal." He said, "When you saw the classes, you just knew that something was very wrong." Eighty percent of the students were in "honors" or other upper-track courses. Nearly all of the students in those classes were white. Twenty percent of the students of Sullins High were in the Regents-level courses. Students in the lower-track classes were described by Patel as primarily "minority students receiving free or reduced-price lunch, special education students, and a handful of white males from blue-collar families." The vast majority of the students in the lower-track English and social studies classes were male and black.

Over the opposition of the former principal who had retired, Superintendent Simons had already planned to consolidate ninth-grade English into one track the year that Patel arrived. Patel recommended expanding detracking to social studies and tenth-grade English as well. He viewed the inequities that he saw as requiring quick interventions. Not only was he appalled by what he saw at Sullins, he saw no reason to delay reform. In his former district, detracking had gone off without a hitch. It was an all-white, upper-middle-class district, and parents viewed the elimination of low-track classes as an expansion of opportunity for their children.

At the same time, Patel was savvy enough to know that his proposal would meet with some resistance. He was not prepared, however, for the ferocity of opposition he encountered, especially from the small but affluent waterfront area of Lyons Bay.

The parents of Lyons Bay wielded most of the power in the district. They turned out the vote for school board elections, put "Support the Budget" signs on their lawns, supported candidates, and were active in the PTAs. Their waterfront homes were the most desirable, and the most expensive, in the district. Many were not shy about reminding the school board about how much their tax bill was. And nearly all of the children of Lyons Bay were in the honors and AP tracks.

When Superintendent Simons began his detracking effort, he set off a firestorm that continued during Patel's first year as principal. At one meeting of the school board, parents from Lyons Bay came out in force. Patel was appalled when he noticed that every member of that parent group was dressed alike, in the same color shirts with the slogan "Stand for Excellence." They appeared to not be cognizant of the signal that they were sending to every parent who came out to support the elimination of the lower track. Although race was never mentioned, the coding of racial prejudice was thinly veiled. Parents referred to "those kids who don't care" and who are "rude and disrespectful." Likewise, they did not hesitate to say that the low-track students had parents "who did not care" and how unfair it was that Simons and Patel wanted to "raise the floor by sacrificing their children's class." Clearly, the parents of Lyons Bay and their allies believed they owned and deserved the honors track.

Because enrollment in honors classes was open to all, based on interest and the maintenance of good grades, all the students who lived in Lyons Bay, with the exception of those with severe learning disabilities, had easy access to the upper track. Their parents were fine with allowing some outsiders in, provided that they behaved and worked hard. The students who did not, deserved, in their minds, to be excluded by being placed in the low-track class, the after-hours school, or in the very large alternative school, where they could receive some education while not impacting their children's education. The achievement gap may have been Simons or Patel's problem, but it was not their problem.

It is not surprising when groups that believe they benefit from the status quo come out in force to protect their advantage. When Amy Stuart Wells and Jeannie Oakes studied ten integrated schools that were undergoing a detracking reform, they observed the same process of protests occurring as each school detracked. They observed how "politically powerful parents of the students who have succeeded and even excelled in the current system are often able to maintain the status quo, despite educational research that suggests that a new system could better serve all students. These powerful parents demand something in return for their commitment to public education—for keeping their children in public schools, as opposed to fleeing to the private schools that many could afford."[4] In the case of Sullins High, there were few private-school options in the area, so the battle, in the minds of the parents who opposed detracking, seemed even more important.

The honors track was in effect a "private" high school within a public high school and they did not want to give it up, despite the evidence Simons and Patel provided showing that detracking would work. When the school leaders would point to the success of neighboring schools, even those with similar demographics, there was always a reason why that school just was not the same as Sullins. Simons heard the same reasoning as Josh Starr had heard in a different state at a different time: Sullins, just like Stamford, was "unique."

As we saw previously, when powerful parents align themselves with powerful teachers of high-track classes, interests in maintaining the status quo converge.

In tracked systems, a considerable amount of power is given to teachers. Disruptive students are often "down-tracked" to remove them from classes. Because track recommendations and grades will vary, not all students have equitable access to honors and AP programs. A poor class-participation grade can mean the difference between getting into an Advanced Placement class or being excluded from it.

At the same time, it is not uncommon for the teachers, counselors, and even administrators to be afraid not to give the children of powerful parents access to high-track classes. Although tracking creates many headaches around the issue of placement, some teachers are reluctant to give up the power of track placement, along with the perks of teaching high-track classes.

Although most of the alliances against tracking were among parents of Sullins High, there were a few teacher/parent alliances. Some honors and AP teachers were still angry over the self-selection program that the district had in place. They liked the old system where they got to decide who took honors and AP courses. They were sure that self-selection had damaged their programs. The thought of opening honors classes to all students made them shudder. Not all teachers, however, were opposed to detracking. Teachers who taught the heterogeneous English 9 classes enjoyed teaching the diverse classes. They had experienced the advantages of detracking, and they did not want to go backwards.

Despite the voices of the powerful, Simons and Patel held their ground. Sol Simons even went so far as to tell the public (and his board of education) that detracking was a decision that was his alone to make. By doing so, he gave the board political cover and established his own authority to continue on with the reform.

During the first two years, Patel began to see positive effects from detracking. Discipline referrals decreased, and the enrollment in tenth-grade AP social studies doubled. Course failures decreased as well. Patel was ready to move on. Unfortunately for him, Simons moved on as well—he was offered another opportunity and he was tired of the battle.

Simons's replacement knew the dangers of detracking, and he was not so keen on moving the reform forward. He was worried that top AP scores might decline, and he had conflicting feelings about expanding access to the school's best classes. In an early conversation with Patel, he even hinted that he might reinstate tracking at the high school.

Thomas Patel was despondent at the thought of seeing his equity initiative unwind. He knew that detracking was the right thing to do in any community, but in a high school like his, it was vital. So he went about quietly extending the reform. He eliminated the after-hours school and reduced the alternative school population by more than half. He eliminated less-rigorous elective classes in science. He detracked foreign language studies. And he listened to the voices of the parents who had opposed the change.

In the first year of the program, parents complained that the literature read by students and the work that was required of them was too easy—it was not at the former honors level of rigor that had existed before. Dr. Patel helped facilitate conversations, especially with the Lyons Bay parents, around the ninth- and tenth-grade English curriculum. The recommendations were taken seriously, and the curriculum was revised. Parents were not able to veto the reforms, but their input was solicited in determining the challenge level of the class. It was a strategy that worked. As Patel proudly told me in a December 2012 conversation, opposition to detracking was no longer an issue at the school.

Patel made other changes as well. He instituted common planning periods for departments, more staff development, school visits, and changes in teaching assignments. He wisely knew that detracking was not a mere technical change in student assignment to classes, it was a change in the mindset of teachers. How they taught would change even as whom they taught was changing.

Patel, whose temperament is both easygoing and kind, was able to push through the resistance of powerful parents without pushing them over. His principles and persistence, even in the first tenuous years of his principalship, made what seemed like the impossible happen. In 2013, however, his push to reduce tracking in grade-ten social studies met with resistance from central administration, even though it had the support of his teachers. Although in the end, the change was instituted, Patel left Sullins for another high school that would be more open to the reforms in which he deeply believed.

QUESTIONING PRIVILEGE IN EVANSTON TOWNSHIP HIGH SCHOOL

School board president Mark Metz was up for reelection in 2011 in the midst of a controversy over the detracked ninth-grade humanities program.[5] He could have easily hedged on his support of detracking the Evanston Township High School, and made the firestorm go away. He did not. "To me it was a matter of right and wrong, and the election made me more resolute," he told me. If Evanston High School was ever going to increase the achievement of all of its students, then every student needed to be challenged, and the school needed to stop "relegating them [low-track students] to lower performance on the way in."

Evanston Township High School has some of the finest facilities in the country. It has a planetarium, a greenhouse, two swimming pools, and computer labs fitted out with the latest technology. Although it is one school, it is its own district, accepting students from the K–8 District 65, which encompasses the integrated city of Evanston and a portion of the village of Skokie. The high school is located on a sixty-five-acre campus in the small city that is the home of Northwestern University. Evanston, Illinois, is a Chicago suburb located on the Lake Michigan shore. The school is known for its outstanding music program, an Intel-recognized program in mathematics, and its SAT scores, which are well above the national average. It is also known, however, for its achievement gap.

Evanston High School is proud of its diversity. Its student body is 45 percent white, 30 percent black, 16 percent Latino, 5 percent mixed race, and 4 percent Asian. Some of its students come from homes supported by more than ample incomes. Yet, 40 percent of its nearly three thousand students receive free or reduced-priced lunch. As in all the cases in this book, its tracks are stratified by race and wealth.

Longtime history teacher David Futransky remembers when there were seven different tracks in some courses ranging from remedial to high honors.[6] He told me that a priest he admired, who was now retired, used to say that Evanston was a town with "drive-by diversity." Although it was technically integrated, the races lived lives apart. That was certainly true in the high school's classrooms. It was as though there were multiple schools under one roof. Since Futransky began, that had changed a little bit. By the time Superintendent Eric Witherspoon arrived, in 2006, the number of tracks in freshman humanities had been reduced to four.

Witherspoon knew that something had to be done to address the achievement gap between the school's white and black and Latino students. And so he decided in 2008 to reduce tracking even further by moving from four levels to three—honors for the top 5 percent, mixed honors for the majority of students, and remedial classes for the students who were below level in reading skills.[7] The hope was that at least the middle track would reflect the school's diversity.

As modest as it was, the plan was not met with universal approval. The community was divided. Some parents did not believe that teachers were capable of keeping standards high in the mixed honors course, and that all of their attention would go to the kids who struggled. A PTSA (parent, teacher, student association) president asked, "What is honors . . . if you take out the middle?"[8] Teachers complained that they were neither prepared nor consulted, warning that if the move from four tracks to three were implemented too quickly it would be a disaster for students.

There were also those who supported the change. The chairwoman of the local NAACP Education Committee, Anne Sills, said that the time had come. The school had to evolve or risk becoming a charter because of its lack of progress under NCLB. ETHS graduate Sills understood the racial dynamics that fueled the opposition to the reduction in tracking. She told the board that detracking would "change the complexion of honors classes."[9] She knew how the four tracks were stratified by race—white students were primarily in the top two and students of color in the bottom two. A twelfth-grade student complained that the proposal did not go far enough. "Tracking limits and segregates our diverse school environment and puts some students on a pedestal for being able to take a test better than others."[10]

That student's observation, regarding how tracking divided the school, was echoed by school board president Martha Burns. Burns noted how Evanston High School operated as if it were two different schools. She asked, "What is it going to take for students of color to be part of this great institution? . . . It's not about going to Homecoming. It's about our children having intellectually stimulating experiences in the core curriculum."[11] After a month of community input and debate, the school board approved the reduction of tracking at the March 2008 meeting. It eliminated "regular" humanities with a unanimous vote, even as some continued to argue that keeping "straight honors" for the students who scored in the top 5 percent of the ACT Explore test was wrong. Veteran English teacher Fred Schenck spoke up: "In my fifteen years here, one thing has become more and more painful each day. This building privileges a certain group of people and that privilege drives the decisions here."[12] The struggle to truly integrate a school and give all students access to challenging learning by overcoming the forces of privilege had begun.

Superintendent Witherspoon knew that the detracking efforts could not end in 2008. He was a veteran superintendent of more than twenty years—having served in two minority districts prior to coming to Evanston. He knew that the gap in curriculum could not continue to exist if his school was ever to be both excellent and equitable. The time when schools were judged to be great based on the performance of only their top students was long gone. For him, detracking the school and supporting its struggling students was a moral imperative. Board president Mark Metz said that making Evanston better for all of its students was the very mission for which Eric Witherspoon had been hired. According to Metz, Witherspoon was both coura-geous and innovative, two necessary characteristics of the kind of leader who would be willing to take on significant school reform, even one that would meet with resistance.

Eric Witherspoon continued to seek support to push the reform forward. History/social science chairperson Jennifer Fisher was an eager ally.[13] For a long time she had been wondering why educators always seemed to assume there are "honors kids" rather than focusing on what it means to do "honors work." She saw too many parents push their students into honors and mixed honors for status, the "bump" they received from taking a weighted course and to avoid "kids who were not serious"—which was code, she suspected, for "minority stu-dents." That became a question she posed to Eric Witherspoon and others—why should honors students be separated from the rest based on test scores? If they were given the opportunity to do honors work, and to continue to push themselves at a higher level, wouldn't that be enough? And if they were in class with other students, wouldn't they inspire others to reach the honors level as well? Honors recognition, she thought, should be based on what you do, not who you are. The big question, "What does it mean to do honors work?" began to guide discussions.

David Futransky, the former teacher union president, agreed—and he could mobilize faculty support. He and other teacher leaders became co-partners in the quest to further detrack the school and give an honors curriculum to all students. Futransky worked with local groups including the NAACP and the YWCA to promote di-alogue across racial lines. In addition, the district formed a school-improvement team in 2009 to both study the progress of mixed-level classes and make recommendations to the superintendent regarding how they could be improved.

Eric Witherspoon believes that when it comes to detracking, it is not enough to simply do what is right, you must do it *right*. Doing it right is what makes reforms work. He put in place a program called

SOS (Systems of Support). Support classes were made available, as was before-school help. The program received positive evaluations and so it seemed logical in the fall of 2010 to move the reform forward and reduce three tracks to two. The "straight honors" course for students who scored in the top 5 percent on the Explore test would be blended with the mixed honors class, and for students who read below the fortieth percentile, there would be a humanities plus support course, to which about fifty students would be assigned. The vast majority of the students who had been in the "straight honors" course were white, making up about 25 percent of the freshman class. According to Associate Principal Marcus Campbell, that is when controversy really erupted.[14] The debate became highly charged, with parents accusing the school of jeopardizing students' education. There were rumblings that the abandonment of the exclusive honors program would cause the professors at Northwestern University who had kids in the Evanston school to leave the district. The president of Northwestern expressed his concern that members of the community who publically identified themselves as liberal were coming out against a democratic school reform.

The board of education held a special meeting during which four scholars from local universities reassured the community that the new humanities course would not hurt honors students and would improve all students' educational experience. The Evanston educators with whom I spoke reported that some community members expressed worries about property values declining. Many who came to the meetings that fall were angry, and accused the board of "dumbing down the school" and holding back the "smart kids." By the time the vote came in December, the parent of two honors students, Mindy Wallis, presented the board with a petition with 442 signatures to stop the move. In her presentation she told the board that she knew a parent who was "dying to bring a lawsuit" against the board, and others who were threatening to take their children out of the high school and to unseat school board members.[15]

As we've seen before with detracking reforms, for many parents, success was viewed as a zero-sum game in which "honors students" would inevitably pay a price when the majority "leveled up." They could not believe that all students could have access to the same curriculum and benefit—if that curriculum was "easy" enough for average students, then their children needed something more challenging. This was the privilege that they were accustomed to, and it was the privilege they wanted to preserve. During one meeting, a parent described the move as "punishing the high achieving students who help save ETHS."[16]

The phrase "students who help save ETHS" speaks volumes. The speaker saw bright children as deserving a reward for attending the public school. Their presence within the system was, in this parent's eyes, a gift to the school that enabled it to have a good reputation. Other students thus benefited from their presence. In return, they should have an exclusive place within the building. This is the essence of privilege.

It is not unusual for parents to argue against more heterogeneous classes when their motivation is to isolate their children from other students who, they believe, are not as "bright." Former Rockville Centre principal Robin Calitri spoke of one parent who referred to such students as "the time wasters." Some parents clearly seek something special to which they believe their child is entitled. At an elementary school PTA meeting in the Rockville Centre School District, a parent questioned Superintendent Bill Johnson as to why there was not a test-in, pull-out program for gifted students like hers. The Rockville Centre Schools' Renzulli-based enrichment program, designed to service the gifts and talents of all students, this parent claimed, was not enough. Superintendent Johnson responded with a simple question: "Who in this room does not have a child who has gifts and talents?" Predictably, not one parent raised their hand. However, the conversation would have been a good deal more difficult if the meeting had been about taking away an existing program. Even though the Evanston High School honors program was being expanded, not eliminated, some parents saw it as the end of an elite program, and they were not happy about it.

Despite the opposition to the reform, Eric Witherspoon held his ground, asking the board to move forward. He again expressed his faith in the school's ability to meet the needs of all students while reducing the gaps in achievement. He said, "It can be done. It can be done at ETHS. If not here, where? If not now, when?"[17] Although a few members expressed their hesitation, the plan received the unanimous approval of the board.

Within three days of the vote, the editorial board of the *Chicago Tribune* jumped into the fray, calling the elimination of the exclusive track at ETHS a "terrible idea" because it put high achievers with students who "wouldn't have qualified for the honors track."[18] The editorial's negative predictions about the reform only reinforced parents' anger and worry.

Witherspoon and his staff worked hard to make sure that the new humanities curriculum was challenging and rigorous. Teachers were an integral part of the process and they built curriculum that sought to answer the question posed by Jennifer Fisher, "What does honors work look like?" Teachers created one grading scale and rubrics to determine student achievement. They discussed procedures and process. They recognized the importance of teamwork in teaching the new curriculum. They were determined to create a curriculum that was accessible to all students while at the same time challenging the school's highest achievers.

Witherspoon continued to expand the SOS student-support program. A Saturday-morning program called the Wildkit Academy was developed using Title I funds.[19] Free to all district students, the academy offers academic tutoring; breakfast is served as an incentive for students to attend. Witherspoon says the supports send the message that "we are here to support you today and every day until the day that you graduate." He continued to reach out to the research community to help the parents understand the equity reforms that needed to take place, and to assess the effectiveness of the new program. A team of external evaluators, which included David Figlio of Northwestern University, would measure the efficacy of the detracked classes using indicators that included ACT Explore scores, AP scores, internal assessments, and student learning growth measurements.

As planned, the year following the humanities reform, the district implemented a new ninth-grade curriculum in biology based on overarching themes or "big ideas" and inquiry-based learning. As with the humanities course, students were able to earn honors credit by doing honors-level work. According to Associate Principal Marcus Campbell, students who read below grade level do not take biology until the sophomore year, so there was no reason to add a lower track. "We have learned a lot about our teachers and how to support them in detracking," he said.

When I spoke to educators from Evanston Township High School, they were eagerly preparing for the following year when they would introduce detracking to tenth-grade history and geometry. They felt positive about the change, and all expressed a deep moral commitment to bringing detracking forward. But the changes planned for 2013–14 had to be delayed. When the recommendation to detrack tenth-grade history and Geometry in Construction was put forward, the board was badly split, and a disappointed administration withdrew its recommendation for earned honors in two courses: Modern World History: Global Perspectives and Geometry in Construction.

The withdrawal of the detracking proposal won the praise of board member Jonathan Baum, who said the following: "I fully agree that it is unsound to extend elements of the freshman restructuring to other grade levels and subjects unless and until our outside evaluation, based on external measures, demonstrate these changes in fact increases [sic] student achievement for students at all ability levels."[20]

School board president Mark Metz made it clear that he believed there was no reason to wait—there had been no evidence that the previous detracking was not working. He felt it best that the school continue with the plan supported by teachers and administrators because what existed was "seriously flawed." During the same meeting, Dr. Figlio and another member of the advisory group assessing the reform reassured the board that there was no reason not to continue the detracking initiative. Those board members opposed to allowing detracking to go forward could not be swayed by the experts, the administration, or their fellow board members. At least for now, further detracking is on hold in Evanston.

OVERCOMING PREJUDICE, POWER, AND PRIVILEGE

The belief that the school is the place where the intellectual wheat should be separated from the chaff is still a quiet undercurrent in many of our schools. When the status quo of tracking is challenged, this belief comes to the surface. Parents who hold high academic ambitions for their children often express the fear that if students with lower achievement are in their child's class, the elite opportunities that they believe their child deserves will be lost. Some parents (and educators) just assume that students who learn differently, or who do not grasp material quickly, will disrupt or slow down learning. They have difficulty understanding why a low-track class might not work because they have never experienced its dynamics, or their expectations for the students in the low-track class are so low, they think that what occurs in such a class is fine and appropriate—for someone else's child, just not for their own.

The justification of such separation, even when it results in segregated classrooms, is often grounded in an idealized vision of school as a meritocracy, and the belief that all students, if they work hard enough, can earn a place in a high-track class. In their minds, the playing field is level enough. The advantages brought by tutoring, enriched childhood experiences, or parenting that knows how to get the most out of the school system—all of these are dismissed as inconsequential.

Some parents and teachers will argue that students with weaker skills will be frustrated and act out in challenging classes, disrupting the learning of high achievers as well as their own learning. This might be true if no accommodations are made for struggling learners. The traditional "talk and chalk" model is not effective for any classes. However, with the introduction of student-centered teaching strategies, differentiation, and support, frustration can be avoided. It is important to be able to explain to parents how that can be accomplished.

The bottom line is this—concerns of the parents of high-track students should not be dismissed out of hand. Every parent has the right and duty to advocate for their children. Schools therefore must be very careful that they do not water down curriculum and that they find ways to challenge all students. When the parents of Sullins High School complained that the curriculum was not challenging enough, Principal Patel listened and he adjusted. The teachers of Evanston High School thought long and hard about what it means to do honors work, and they created a curriculum that would both inspire and support that level of student commitment.

The prejudice that must be dealt with when a school detracks often goes beyond these concerns, however. The principal of New England Country School faced far less resistance than the resistance faced by the other two school leaders. Detracking reforms are the most difficult to accomplish in racially integrated schools in which tracking has resulted in de facto segregation in classes, especially when there is a bimodal population, as is the case in Evanston.[21]

Because members of the community were willing to come out and talk about the racial stratification that was caused by tracking, there was a strong countervailing pressure to that exerted by the primarily white parents whose students were in the "straight honors" track. Powerful voices on the issue were not equal, but there was some balance.

To pretend that the "three P's"—power, prejudice, and privilege—do not exist is to ensure that your detracking efforts will fail. Unless you are building a detracked school from the ground up, discussions about these factors must be part of the planning, as well as community education. Evanston's superintendent continually brought in university resources to lead such discussions. Josh Starr created a middle school reform committee that took the time to read and study the effects of tracking. Even if a school cannot afford to bring in a consultant, discussions around data are often enough to make community and staff members take notice of tracking's inequities.

A wide array of data can be used to analyze the effects of tracking, including:

> Demographic data—the proportions of student groups in each class level or track by race, ethnicity, and/or socioeconomic status.

> Resource data—data describing the outside resources available to students, such as access to tutors, music lessons, summer programs, and SAT prep courses.

> Teaching data—data about the years of experience and educational credentials of teachers by course and/or track level.[22]

When study groups carefully review data, as they did in Stamford, Connecticut, they start to see the complexity of the issue as well as the gaps that tracking produces. Carefully guided discussions can help teachers and parents understand why tracking is not the meritocracy that it appears to be.

Be prepared, however, for the "go fix it" arguments. No matter how carefully reformers lead the discussion, those who support tracking will insist that the tracking system can be improved and made more equitable, and therefore that there is no need to eliminate it. They will, as in the case of Evanston, beg the school board to wait for the study to come in. Or, as was the case in Stamford, say that as long as grouping is "flexible" it is not doing any harm. Or, as a parent in Rockville Centre argued, "Fix the curriculum and raise the ceiling for every child."

Defenders of tracking will put outlandish demands on administration. Before signing on to a detracking reform, Evanston School Board member Jonathan Baum wanted to see the data showing that all students would have their achievement go up as a result.[23] That the present system created racially stratified classes was not seen as a matter for sufficient concern.

The bottom line is that no matter how hard a school may try, tracking cannot be reformed or "fixed," although many schools have attempted to do just that. As stated previously, the National Research Council felt so strongly about tracking's ineffectiveness, it concluded that students should not be educated in low-track classes due to the overwhelmingly negative research regarding them.[24]

After reading about the struggles encountered by those who seek to detrack their schools, readers may be asking themselves, is detracking worth it? It is a reasonable question, because the road is never smooth, and resistance is certain. It is far easier to add tracks, for example, than to take them away. When tracks are added, they are seen as an additional service. Perhaps it is smaller class size for a remedial class. Perhaps it is the status of exclusivity of access to a high-track class. Perhaps it is the label of "gifted and talented," which enhances parental pride. There are not many parents who understand, as Wendy Lecker did, that "the service" comes at a price—especially for low-track students.[25]

So why, then, would a school leader, teacher, or parent take the risk and challenge the status quo? Detracking is all about leadership. The connected leadership of the school board, superintendent, assistant superintendent, and principals was key to Rockville Centre's success. Later, administrative and teacher leadership in South Side High School helped carry the reform forward.

The leadership of the superintendents of Woodland Hills and Stamford was key to progress in those districts. The leadership of a principal in Sullins garnered support among teachers. The leadership of Evanston was broad and included a board president, superintendent, community leaders, and teachers. The hope is that the good effects that result from detracking are enough to sustain it when the leaders leave. Sometimes that happens, and other times (as in the case of Woodland Hills) it does not.

And yet, despite the stories of resistance and even the negative impact that detracking has had on some careers, school leaders continue to look to detracking as a strategy for school improvement. Rarely is the leader who pushes the reform naive regarding the risks. Even as a belief system operates to block detracking, a competing system compels educators to move forward.

The stories in this chapter, and throughout this book, demonstrate that it is possible to overcome the political objections to detracking, even if it is a slow road and an incomplete one. Courage and patience are invaluable assets. However, understanding that tracking is not a technical change, but a reform that questions beliefs about learning and human potential, is the first step in a successful process. Detracking makes us question the very purpose of schooling, beyond test scores, group labels, and student schedules. It asks us to think about what the good society looks like, and it compels us to make our schools and classrooms reflect what we know in our hearts it should be.

9

Lessons Learned and the Reforms of Today

As noted in the introduction, when I first contemplated writing this book I worried that everything that needed to be said about tracking had already been said. The political pressures and normative beliefs that impeded detracking efforts decades ago in Woodland Hills, Pennsylvania, are the same ones now operating in Evanston, Illinois. As the old adage goes, the more things change, the more they stay the same.

However, as I researched the subject and conducted interviews for this book, I realized that the recurrent beliefs, themes, and narratives associated with each story of detracking were exactly what made telling these stories so important. First, despite all the known obstacles, school leaders, parents, and teachers are still willing to fight the battle to detrack schools. There is a logic and an optimism to detracking that captures the minds, souls, and hearts of those who are concerned with equitable learning opportunities for all students, and thus there are leaders willing to take on the challenge. Because of that impulse toward equity, schools will continue to look to detracking as a solution. Many will succeed—perhaps not to the extent of banishing tracking practices completely—but their reforms will create better schools. It is my hope that the research and anecdotes provided in this book will prove helpful to their success.

APPLYING WHAT WE KNOW ABOUT TRACKING TO TODAY'S SCHOOL REFORMS

There is a second compelling purpose, however, that this book serves at this moment in time. The research on tracking—looking at factors such as peer effects, the effects of racial isolation on student achievement, student ability grouping, and track assignment by score or by choice, as well as the normative and political forces that sustain tracking—can serve as a lens through which we examine current school-change initiatives. The beliefs and problems associated with tracking also apply to many of the reform initiatives popular today. We find them in school choice, test-in schools, charters, and teacher evaluation by student test scores. If we fail to intervene, we can expect the same inequities associated with tracking to occur on a wider scale.

School Choice

School choice is premised on the belief that the forces of the marketplace—choice and competition—are the best drivers of school improvement.[1] Most researchers credit economist Milton Friedman with applying the concept of choice to the realm of education. In the 1950s, Friedman began to advance the argument that the laws of supply and demand would improve school quality. He pushed vouchers (tax dollars given to parents to use toward private school tuition) as a means of giving more students access to better schools. Since that time, "school choice" has expanded to include public and private charter schools, online schools, public school inter- and intra-district choice, virtual schools, and homeschooling. Advocates of choice include neoliberals who want community alternatives to the local public school, to conservatives who wish to infuse the forces of the marketplace into schooling with the hope of driving down costs and increasing school quality. In addition, choice appeals to libertarians who believe that they have the right to choose curriculum, school type, and whatever else they think is best for their child without the interference of the government.

Choice is popular with those who hold a functionalist perspective of schooling, which is based on the premise that schools are responsible only for the achievement (defined by test scores) of the students attending them. Parents make good choices or bad choices as to where their children are educated, and children live with the consequences. This is very different from the perspective that sees the providing of equality of opportunity for *all* students—not only those in choice schools, but those left behind as well—to be a public responsibility.

For example, those who advocate for charters will cite the achievement gains of the students in a successful charter school as evidence for why there should be more charters. They do not cite the evidence of charters that fail miserably or have worse gains than the local public school. They are not concerned with the effect that charters or other alternative schools have when they pull higher-scoring students and highly motivated students, along with funding, from the local public school. In that regard they are similar to the parents of high-track students who, when confronted with the evidence of the negative effects of low-track classes, simply tell the district to "fix the low-track."

School choice has been in existence long enough for us to study its effects on racial stratification and student achievement. In 2001, researchers from the University of Colorado examined the results of choice policies on student achievement, school diversity, and equitable access in the Boulder Valley School District.[2] Boulder Valley introduced choice in 1961, although it was not widely used by parents until the 1990s. Overall, they found that choice did not increase student achievement—where some schools saw enhanced results, others realized a decline. Schools, like students assigned to tracks, were either winners or losers as a result of choice policies. Choice resulted in "skimming"; that is, the top students fled from their neighborhood school to the top schools. The top schools had lower shares of minority and poor students. Meanwhile, charter schools that were designed for higher achievers gained higher-achieving students, resulting in the further increase of their scores. According to the Boulder Valley study, a vicious cycle began. In schools with higher numbers of minority students, white students with higher test scores left, school test scores went down, and the percentage of students receiving free or reduced-price lunch increased, which in turn caused even more students to flee. In one school in the district, white students left at a rate that was two times their proportion in the school. In the 20 percent of schools that had the lowest proportion of white students (median of 68 percent), white enrollment declined to 44 percent in a period of six years.

In short, the schools in Boulder Valley, Colorado, became more stratified by race and SES because of choice. Choosing schools, just like choosing tracks, resulted in stratification. The share of special needs students in schools shifted as well. The "new mission" schools most associated with elitism had student special education populations as low as 3.6 percent, while a high school for vocational education had a special education population of a remarkably disproportionate 26 percent.

Although in theory every student can choose, the authors of the Boulder report note that in reality, choice is more complicated. Parents must visit the school, provide transportation for their child to and from school, and in some cases contribute "sweat equity"; that is, volunteer to do work at the school. Schools have the ability to reject some students with disabilities if they cannot accommodate their needs. In addition, in order to be admitted to some charter schools, the student applicant had to be enrolled in a tuition-based preschool. Such policies limited who could freely participate in choice.

The authors of the Boulder Valley study concluded that it appeared the effect on student achievement was a "zero-sum game"—although choice resulted in some schools' scores increasing, it appeared to be at the expense of other schools' scores decreasing as high-achieving students fled the school. They further concluded that "culling academic achievement out as a special need that may be used to define the mission of certain BVSD schools has resulted in tracking writ large—tracking between schools rather than within them."[3] In other words, by saying that "giftedness" or, on the other hand, learning English as a second language, is a special need that can only be met if all students have that same academic profile, the district created schools which are, at their essence, tracks.

The tracking research on peer effects informs our understanding of how the movement of students of varying achievement among schools is important not only to overall school achievement, but to the achievement of students in the receiving school. Even as we know that peer effects influence achievement in classrooms, so do peer effects influence the achievement of an entire school. A study of the effects of student movement after Hurricane Katrina provides important insights.

Following the hurricane, the students of the hardest-hit areas were displaced from their homes and schools and sent to schools across Louisiana and Texas. Five thousand New Orleans students enrolled in the Houston Independent School District. In 2009, three researchers conducted a study on the effects of the influx of students on those students already in the Houston schools.[4] Some of the Houston schools had an influx of lower-achieving students from New Orleans, while others had an influx of high achievers. The authors found that an influx of lower-achieving students into a school hurt the achievement of all native Houston students, especially students with low skills in elementary schools, and students with higher achieve-ment in secondary schools. The opposite was true for the entrance of high-achieving students into Houston schools. The influx of high achievers into a particular school benefited all the native Houston students—especially the low-achieving ones. As in the classroom study of peer effects discussed earlier in this book, low-achieving stu-dents are most affected by the influence of their peers and will learn more if stronger students are in the class, and less if surrounded by other low-achieving students.

The above findings are important because they indicate an un-intended consequence of choice. As students move between schools, not only is their own achievement affected, the achievement of other students in the receiving school is as well. Not only are schools "win-ners and losers"—so are the students who attend them.

The stratification effects of choice are not limited to the Boulder Valley School District—they exist in other choice systems as well. The Brookings Institution considers New York City to have the most effective school-choice system of any major city in the United States because it gives parents both freedom and options when choosing a school. Those options are limited by the sorting and selection of the schools.

The process does not end with parent and student choice—the school must also choose the student, and the student needs an advo-cate to help her choose wisely. Although in 2003 the city attempted to reform the choice system so that it would be fairer to all students in the city, the effort fell short. According to a report by the New School's Center for New York City Affairs, there are serious flaws in the choice system. For example, students who do not have a strong parent advocate who can help them navigate the applications and the tours are left to find their way in a complicated system. Some fourteen thousand students, according to the report, are assigned to high schools that they did not choose—half of these students were rejected by all of their choices. They are then assigned and clustered in some of the lowest-performing high schools in the city, in schools already overwhelmed with high-needs students.[5]

This negative effect of choice is well known to the Department of Education of the City of New York. In 2006, the department received a report from a consulting firm, the Parthenon Group, with which it had contracted to study city graduation rates and how they might be improved.[6]

In the report, Parthenon clearly demonstrated the relationship between the percentage of high-risk students, which Parthenon defined as overage and undercredited (OA-UC) for their grade level, and the graduation rates of the city's high schools. They provided the evidence that students who entered high school with low test scores were more likely to become an OA-UC student. Certainly this finding is not surprising, and on the surface might appear to have little to do with choice.

Yet the connection between the above and the city's choice policies is demonstrated in Parthenon's additional findings regarding the effects of the *proportion* of low-scoring students in any given high school. According to the study, the concentration of high school students whose eighth-grade scores were below proficiency explains 22 percent of the variation in graduation outcomes for students whose eighth-grade scores were Level 1 or Level 2.[7] Students who had a Level 2 score (below proficiency) in either math or ELA experienced the most dramatic negative effects if they were in schools with large shares of OA-UC students. In short, in schools with disproportionate numbers of low-scoring students, the school becomes one big low-track class, and all of the issues associated with low-track classes apply to the school, thus increasing the chances that its students become OA-UC and eventually drop out. Unlike the Houston study, however, the few Level 3 (proficient) and Level 4 (above proficient) students in those schools did not have a drop in their graduation prospects.

In 2008, Parthenon issued a draft follow-up report comparing the graduation prospects of students with a score of 2.5 and a significantly lower score of 2.0. If the student *with the lower score* attended a smaller school with a more academically diverse student body, similar to the average city high school, the chance of his or her graduation was 2 percentile points higher than the student with the superior initial test score.[8] In other words, proximity to higher-scoring peers trumped prior achievement in its effects on graduation rates. Clearly, the warehousing of low-achieving students in large high schools was contributing to the dropout rate, and choice was part of the problem. The consulting group advised the city to more evenly disperse high-risk students throughout the system, using controlled choice.

There are other equity issues associated with choice beyond the above. The present choice system in New York City is both elaborate and complex. Middle school students and their parents are required to navigate a system of four hundred high schools in deciding which to attend. Students rank up to twelve schools or programs within schools. A computer program then uses the student ranking of schools and the schools' ranking of students to create "matches." A study by Sean P. Corcoran, of New York University, and Henry M. Levin, of Columbia's Teachers College, describes the complexity of the system.[9]

Corcoran and Levin explain the variety of school types as well as their differing entrance criteria. Unscreened schools are based on lottery admission. Zoned schools give priority to students who live in the neighborhood. Educational Option ("ED Opt") schools require a more academically diverse population—enrolling students of higher, average, and lower achievement. Limited unscreened schools give priority to students who attend an informational session or open house.

The most coveted schools are the ones that are highly selective in their admissions. These are test-in schools, which base admissions on one standardized test, and screened and audition schools that have their own screening process, which includes criteria such as grades, seventh-grade test scores, essays, exams, attendance, and open-house visits.

Prior to the present choice policies, most of the choice schools were ED Opt. They were schools that gave families choice, but required a more academically diverse population in the school—in line with the recommendations of the Parthenon Group. In 2005, there were more ED Opt schools than any other—about 250. By 2010, screened schools and limited unscreened schools, which have no academic balancing requirements, dramatically rose while ED Opts declined by 25 percent.

New York City schools are now under fewer obligations to recruit students with high needs. And because of the aggressive school-closing policies, schools are leery of doing so. In a 2011 analysis, entitled *Programmed to Fail: The Parthenon Report and Closing Schools*, Jackie Bennett pointed out that rather than creating policies that would explicitly admit high-risk students into newly created schools, as the Parthenon report suggested, high-needs students often wound up concentrated in older schools that were already being overwhelmed by high concentrations of similar students. Sometimes, Bennett notes, small schools, with far fewer high-needs students, were even in the very same building. In her article, Bennett links the resulting concentrations, with the policy of closing failing schools.[10]

In the current climate, in which both the principals and teachers of New York City are evaluated in part by the test scores of their students, there are even greater incentives to recruit students with good attendance and good grades and to avoid students with poor attendance, grades, and scores. The effect of teacher and principal evaluation on such issues will be discussed later in this chapter.

In light of these reports, how have policies changed? Unfortunately, rather than delving deeply into all of the ways that selection policies affect schools and student success, there is still a strong tendency to deflect the issue by finding schools that outperform others with what are, at least on the surface, similar student populations. The Parthenon Group's 2008 update also presented statistics on what they called "beat the odds" schools; that is, schools whose graduation rates were better than they were expected to be. The report, however, provided little detail on how these schools were actually compared to one another. In addition, when 2005 data were compared with 2007 data, only 35 percent of the "beats the odds" schools had continued high performance. The percentage of schools that had either improved or declined was roughly the same percentage as those that continued to outperform. Observing that some of the "beat-the odds" schools are designed for recent immigrants, Bennett noted that "by the nature of their demographics, these schools are able to focus very specifically on a defined need. And because they consistently beat the odds—there may very well be a socio-economic (demographic) factor at work within the recent-immigrant population that is unaccounted for in the usual formulas DoE uses to give us evidence of school success."[11]

The narrative of the "beat the odds" school started more than a decade ago with Kati Haycock of Education Trust, known for her fast-paced PowerPoint-driven lectures on schools that had extraordinary test scores.[12] It coincided with the beginnings of No Child Left Behind and reinforced the message that gaps needed to be exposed and that this exposure, along with the setting of test-score goals, would result in higher achievement for all. That message is appealing to neoliberal and neoconservative reformers because it neatly shifts the blame from systemic problems like resources, poverty, racial isolation, and choice, to teachers and principals. If one school is outstanding, surely all schools should be. It also shifts the work. In the present climate, unwinding choice, desegregating schools and neighborhoods, and providing more resources to schools with high-needs students are not politically popular positions.

Screened and Test-in Schools

The following examples show how selection processes act like tracking, affecting not only educational outcomes, but also the demographics of the school population in New York City schools.

Aviation Career and Technical Education High School is a school that selects its incoming students. It is a screened school, with the individual programs each having their own entrance criteria. The average score of incoming Aviation students is 3.18, well above the city average of 2.68 on the four-point scale. Only 7 percent of its incoming students are black, well below the city average of 30 percent. Twenty-seven percent of its students are Asian American, nearly twice the city average of 15 percent. Only 5 percent of its students are special education students.

Automotive High School is another technical education high school, which, partially because it is not a screened school, serves a very different population of students. At Automotive, the average incoming score is 2.49, below the city average. Sixty-six percent of its students are black, while only 1 percent are Asian American. The special education rate is a whopping 30 percent.

The 2011 four-year graduation rate of the screened tech school was 88 percent, while the rate for the unscreened school was only 52 percent. Secretary of Education Arne Duncan visited Aviation High School in 2013 and sang the praises of career and technical education. He did not mention that the school did not match the demographic makeup of the students of the city, nor did he mention that students needed to apply to get in.

Certainly the most selective are the city's test-in schools such as Stuyvesant High School and the Bronx High School of Science. As noted in chapter 3, admission to the eight elite specialized high schools in New York City is based on one factor—a test known as the Specialized High School Admissions Test. Less than 6 percent of the black and Latino students who took the test were offered a seat in one of the eight schools, while more than 25 percent of all white test takers and nearly 35 percent of all Asian students were offered a seat.[13] That single entrance criterion has become the basis of an NAACP complaint filed with the US Department of Education. In a complex system of test-in schools, screened schools, audition schools,

Ed Opt schools, limited unscreened schools, unscreened schools, and zone schools, it is no wonder that choice has resulted in the same stratification that results from tracking. New York City is the third-most-segregated large-city school system in the nation, behind only Chicago and Dallas.[14]

The lawsuit regarding test-in schools described above is not the only legal complaint filed against the choice system. In May of 2013, Wendy Lecker, senior attorney at the Campaign for Fiscal Equity Project of the Education Law Center in New York, filed a complaint on behalf of parents and community groups with the US Department of Education's Office of Civil Rights.[15] Ms. Lecker is the parent who played such a vital role in the detracking of Stamford Public Schools, discussed in an earlier chapter. The complaint claims that the high school admissions policy and practices results in the creation of schools with high concentrations of high-needs students, and that black and Latino students are overwhelmingly consigned to such schools, thus lowering their chances of graduation.

The complaint makes the case that since the Parthenon report of 2006, the Department of Education of New York City has been well aware of the problem but has failed to provide any remedy. According to the complaint, the forty schools that have the highest proportion of overage students are more than 90 percent black and/or Latino. The forty-two schools with the lowest concentrations of overage students are disproportionately white. Similarly, 93 percent of the forty schools with the lowest scores of incoming students are more than 90 percent minority. According to the complaint, "the lower the average entering score the more likely the school is to be a Minority School."[16]

As in New York City, the school-choice and selection policies of Buffalo, New York, have resulted in the warehousing of the highest-needs children in high schools with abysmally low graduation rates: in this case, below 40 percent. Six Buffalo schools have become the repositories for all of the students who don't meet the admission requirements for the city's other high schools. Reporting on these six schools, which are being targeted for interventions or takeover, the *Buffalo Times* described extraordinarily high percentages of students who did not speak English, and one school in which the rate of students with learning disabilities reached 33 percent. Commenting on how the school-choice system had led to the problem, the newspaper quoted parent activist Samuel Radford III, who observed, "We're segregating our students based on academic performance." Radford went on to describe the district's placement policies as a "caste system" and "stacked deck."[17]

In their overview of the research on choice systems and segregation, Roslyn Mickelson and colleagues found the same patterns existing nationwide.[18] They conclude that rather than promoting diversity, choice systems are just as segregated as or even more segregated by race and class than the community public schools. Reasons for this include: the design of the school (for example, intention to serve the gifted, the artistic, low-SES students), schools informally choosing students (for example, limiting access to ELL or special education services, strict discipline codes), scarcity of choice beyond the community, and parental preferences for schools with demographic characteristics like their own, regardless of school test scores. Without deliberate attempts to include policies that diversify schools by race, class, and achievement, as some magnets and ED Opt schools do, choice is little more than tracking writ large.

Charter Schools

Charter schools are also in vogue as a mechanism for school reform. The original mission of charter schools was to serve as spaces for innovation and experimentation in order to create practices for replication in public schools. It was also hoped that the competition engendered by having a charter in the neighborhood would spur the local public school to improve.

Charter schools originally were designed to serve students who struggled to be successful in schools. They were encouraged to open in neighborhoods where the local public school was struggling. Charters receive public funding and also use private donations to fund operation. But charter schools and their mission have vastly expanded. Private, for-profit charter schools also now operate in some states.

Although a full description and evaluation of charters is beyond the scope of this book, it is important to note that the most comprehensive evaluation of charters, conducted by the Center for Research on Education Outcomes (CREDO) at Stanford University, found small differences in student performance between charter schools and public schools.[19] Like public schools, charters vary in quality and in student outcomes.

Some of the dynamics associated with tracking also are relevant, however, to how we should evaluate the consequences of the presence of charters. Charter schools are, overall, more segregated by race and class than the local public schools, and enroll a lower percentage of special education and English-language learners.[20] According to a 2010 report by the Civil Rights Project, 70 percent of black students and 50 percent of Latino students who attend charter schools are in intensely segregated schools, in which 90–100 percent of the students are black or Latino. This occurs in part because there is evidence that parents choose like-race charters for their children, regardless of school achievement.[21] Duke University researchers found that charter schools are far more likely to be unbalanced by race than public schools. In North Carolina, 30 percent of public school students in North Carolina attend a school that is racially unbalanced (more than 80 percent white/Asian or black/Latino); however, more than 60 percent of charter school students attend a racially unbalanced school.[22]

There is also evidence to suggest that charter schools are functioning as "white flight" havens—providing elite education that draws white students out of integrated public schools. A recent court case brought by the Little Rock Arkansas School District and others argued that the newly opened charters of Pulaski County were similar to a previous attempt at creating a splinter school district designed to further segregate the Little Rock Schools, which are under court supervision for past segregation practices.[23] The case was brought because charters are pulling a disproportionate number of white and wealthier students from the district schools. Although the judge would not grant the Little Rock District the unitary status it sought, he did not find that the charter schools should be prohibited as an impediment to desegregation. There is concern that this ruling will further spur the creation of charters designed to appeal to white parents of Little Rock.[24]

Little Rock is not alone. The Pataula Charter Academy in Edison, Georgia, draws students from a five-county region of the state with high poverty. In the public schools in the county where the charter is located, white students comprise 2 percent of the student body. However, 75 percent of the charter's students are white, and the number of students who receive free or reduced-price lunch is considerably lower than in the public schools.[25]

Charters have also been repeatedly accused of skimming (taking the strongest students from the local public schools). Although it may be true in many cases, most studies do not find a discernible difference in entering student scores. However, because charters do not offer expensive services in special education and English-language acquisition, there is research that demonstrates that market-oriented charter schools are "cropping off" services to students whose needs make them most costly and more difficult to educate, thus reducing their numbers in charters and increasing their proportion in local public schools.[26] Certainly, the data on lower overall special education and ELL enrollment in charters would suggest that is the case.

There are further concerns that the strict discipline policies that result in higher rates of suspension and expulsion in the charter schools push out the most disruptive students, sending them back to the neighborhood school. In Washington, DC, for example, charter schools, which enroll less than half of all DC students, expelled

676 students, while the public schools expelled only 24 students in a three-year period.[27] In addition, the first-year report of the CEO Leadership Academy of the city of Milwaukee lists an expulsion rate of 27 students of a total student population of only 165. Students are expelled for offenses such as fighting, rule breaking, and possession of contraband—offenses that would likely result in a few days' suspension in public schools. An additional 11 students transferred out of the charter to other schools or to Job Corps.[28]

Mike Petrilli, president of the Thomas B. Fordham Institute, sees the expulsion of misbehaving students from charters as perfectly acceptable in protecting the rights of "educational strivers," whom he believes have been shortchanged by equity initiatives.[29] Petrilli, a tracking advocate, admits that charters do engage in the practice of skimming, which he argues is necessary to meet the needs of the motivated and striving. As for what is to be done for those left behind or pushed out, Petrilli says he is willing to accept less favorable outcomes for these students if it helps their high-achieving peers. The primacy of the needs of the "boy with the purple tie" underpins arguments in favor of choice and charter advocacy.

The African American journalist Natalie Hopkinson sees charters as a sorting system to be avoided. In a 2013 essay in the *Washington Post*, she explains why she would not send her children to a charter, nor would she recommend charter schools to parents whose children "look like mine." She states, "The franchise approach to urban school reform raises some uncomfortable questions about class, race and community. It is creating two permanent tracks of schooling: one for the wealthy and one for the black and brown, and poor."[30]

Hopkinson recognizes that the isolation of students in charters is not the only problem. The tone and practices of charter schools like those in the national KIPP (Knowledge Is Power Program) chain, are more akin to the "drill and skill" practices of low-track classes than to the enriched educational environment of the high-track classroom.

Teacher Evaluation by Test Scores

When NCLB began, I was a supporter. I naively believed that it would, by exposing gaps in achievement, make the nation seriously consider equity initiatives like detracking. Surely the nation would see the differences in the experiences between the haves and have-nots and address the underlying issues of inequitable access to excellence.

I was wrong. Rather than focus on systemic issues of equity— equitable funding, support services for students, racially isolated schooling, and, of course, grouping practices—the focus has been on data outcomes—the test scores. In the world of "corporate school reform," test scores are akin to bottom-line profit. Sanctions such as closing schools and red marks on school report cards became the strategy for improvement. And when the sanctions against organizations and districts did not work, the focus of attention turned to the individual teacher.

According to research, nearly all of which was based on elementary school data, teachers account for about 10 percent to 15 percent of the variance in student test scores.[31] That makes teachers the biggest *in-school* contributor to student learning growth. Out-of-school factors such as poverty and prior achievement play a far greater role in influencing school variance, while other in-school factors such as class size, school spending, and the leadership of the principal influence scores as well.

Nevertheless, improving the quality of teachers has become a major focus of school reform. Policymakers decided that the problem of variation in teacher quality was a problem of evaluation. It has been argued that if we standardized and intensified teacher evaluation and then sorted teachers into groups such as ineffective, effective, and highly effective, we could dismiss the ineffective and provide financial rewards to the highly effective, and thus teaching and learning would improve. The "sort and select" approach underlying tracking was now to be applied to teacher-evaluation systems, and just as in early tracking systems, scores would play a big role in identification.

This was because President Obama's "Race to the Top" reform initiative embraced the idea that a fair and reliable way to evaluate teachers is by student test scores. As part of the attempt to secure Race to the Top funding, states were mandated to create teacher-evaluation plans, in which student growth on standardized tests (generally value-added measures, or VAM scores) play a significant role.[32] Some states chose to count student growth for as much as 50 percent of the teacher's evaluation.

The idea that we can effectively evaluate teachers by means of student test scores rests on two fundamental assumptions. The first is that we can now accurately capture the effect of teachers on student performance. The second assumption is that teacher performance naturally falls on a bell curve, and if we dismiss those at the bottom and reward those at the top, all will be motivated to work harder and the "curve" will shift to the right, leading to better learning outcomes for students.

There are, however, serious flaws in this reasoning. Value-added measures (VAM) of teacher effectiveness do not produce stable or reliable ratings of teachers. They depend on insignificant fluctuations in test scores with a small sample size (a typical class of twenty-five to thirty-five students). This was very apparent in the publication of the teacher data reports in New York City that were used to rank teachers by student test scores. One middle school teacher had his ranking drop from the eighty-eighth percentile in 2009 to the thirty-eighth percentile in 2010.[33] An elementary school teacher in Brooklyn was rated in the sixth percentile when the average performance level of children in her class dropped from 3.97 out of 4.5 on the third-grade test to 3.92 out of 4.5 on the fourth-grade test. Similar problems were found after the publication of teacher ratings in Los Angeles.[34]

What was observed in both of these cities was in fact predictable. Different statistical models (all based on reasonable assumptions) yield different effectiveness scores. Further, research tells us that how a teacher is rated changes from class to class, from year to year, and even from test to test.[35]

It will also come as no surprise to readers that there is bias in the resulting scores depending upon who is in the class or in the school. The shortcomings of evaluating teachers by test scores were apparent in the recent report of the American Institutes for Research (AIR), which developed the New York growth score model.[36] The AIR report explained how as the proportion of students with disabilities and students of poverty in a class or school increases, the average teacher or principal growth score decreases. In short, the larger the share of such students, the more the teacher and principal are disadvantaged by the model.

Likewise, in the 2012 New York model, teachers with students whose prior test scores were higher were advantaged, while teachers whose students had lower prior achievement were disadvantaged. This is in part the result of peer effects, observed in the literature since the 1980s and discussed throughout this book. Without a control for peer effects, we will see patterns of low scores for teachers of disadvantaged students. Over time, the students who have the greatest need for quality teachers and principals may likely see those faculty leave their schools in order to escape the "ineffective" label.[37] This is not unlike the pattern traditionally seen in tracking systems, of the most skilled teachers being assigned to the higher-track classes. In this case, the teachers and principals themselves might seek to leave challenging schools when they can to avoid the "low-track, ineffective" label, which, in many cases they will receive based at least in part on the bias inherent in the scores.

Although most of the research on value-added and growth models as a means by which to evaluate teachers has used elementary data from federally mandated testing, some researchers have looked at teacher evaluation by VAM scores at the secondary level. Predictably, the elephant in the research room was tracking.

Tracking itself appears to confound the teacher effects attributed with value-added scores. C. Kirabo Jackson, of Northwestern University, conducted a comprehensive study of the effects of tracking on the value-added scores of high school teachers.[38] The data for the study were the end-of-course test scores for five cohorts of students in Algebra I and English I. Nearly four hundred thousand North Carolina students had data included in the database. When the researcher included track-level treatment as a variable in the model, he could find no significant teacher effects in English and only slight effects in algebra.

The author concluded that the effects of tracking were so large that "using test scores to identify effective teachers may have limited practical benefits at the high-school level."[39] Further, not accounting for the effects of tracks can lead to an overestimation of teacher effects by 50 percent in algebra and in English. However, when tracks are accounted for, factors other than the teacher's effectiveness, such as students' prior scores, SES, and ELL status can explain all of the variation in scores.

Doug Harris and Andrew Anderson came to a similar finding when they analyzed value-added scores attributed to middle school teachers.[40] They explored how much of the variation in teacher scores was the result of selection bias resulting from the assignment of middle school teachers to different tracks. They found that if tracks were not accounted for, there were large biases in the teacher value-added data. According to the researchers, a teacher who teaches all low-track classes, and is rated in the fiftieth percentile, would see her value-added rating increase to the ninety-ninth percentile if she were given all high-track classes to teach.

The research on the effects of tracking on value-added scores is important for two reasons. First, it is but one more indication of the powerful effects of tracking on students. If it is true that the teacher of the lower track is disadvantaged, and that the disadvantage comes from the lower growth in scores of the students in her class, even after holding students' prior achievement, SES, and other factors constant, then clearly low-track classes have a deleterious effect on the learning growth of the students assigned to the classroom.

Second, it is one more indication of both the futility and the danger of using student test scores to evaluate teachers. Not only is there bias even after attempting to control for student demographics and prior achievement, this effect provides a powerful incentive for teachers to want to teach high-track classes, and for schools to safeguard their best teachers from poor VAM scores by placing them with high-track students.

All in all, this is further evidence that tracking has profound and unequal effects on student learning and that using VAM to ascertain teacher effectiveness is unsound and may result in unintended consequences for students. Rather than improving the educational opportunities of our most at-risk students, the use of VAM in evaluations may actually result in poorer opportunities and thus poorer learning outcomes.

MARKET-BASED VERSUS DEMOCRATIC REFORM: MOVING FROM RESEGREGATION TO EQUITY

As noted in the opening chapter of this book, tracking in schools began at the turn of the twentieth century in response to the influx of immigrants from southern and eastern Europe and the economic imperatives of the industrial era. To serve the needs of the workforce, public schools began sorting students into tracks based on projected life stations.

In the early decades of the twenty-first century, many of the same conditions continue to drive education reform. Schools are changing demographically. The proportion of students of color has increased, and in many schools white students are no longer the majority. Students of color and of poverty are the "new immigrants," and as their numbers rise, so too, it seems, do sorting practices. Our schools are becoming more, not less, segregated, and school-choice initiatives are accelerating that process. Efforts to detrack schools in order to provide equitable opportunities for all children are met with resistance as concerns linger that in "leveling up" our classrooms, "gifted children" will be left behind.

Like the "efficiency" reforms of a century ago that gave rise to school tracking, today's reforms emanate in large part from the business world. Billionaires such as Bill and Melinda Gates, the Walton family, and Eli Broad fund research, think tanks, charter schools, and teacher-evaluation and choice initiatives. They seek to align school practices with business practices such as competition and free-market incentives. Their personal beliefs drive the agenda. The profit motive plays a substantial role. Rupert Murdoch announced that public education is a $500 billion market waiting to be transformed, even as he created the data systems to make that transformation possible.[41]

For market-based reformers, the data provided by student testing is key to school success, to be analyzed like profit margins. These data can be used to sort and select students and teachers. Students' scores determine if they are on the path to college and career readiness. Teachers are evaluated based on changes in these scores from year to year, and rewarded for improvement or sanctioned for decline.

There are already sure signals, however, that "college and career readiness" is morphing into "college *or* career readiness," and that vocational tracking is being revived under the new designation "career and technical education" (CTE). In an opinion piece in the *Albany Times Union*, Kevin Welner and I looked at the history of vocational education in the United States, and why we should be cautious of the resurgence of vocational tracking in public schools. We remind readers that it was at the turn of the last century that Clark University president and psychologist G. Stanley Hall characterized the majority of high school students as part of a "great army of incapables" who should be consigned to schools for "dullards." The social Darwinism that Hall espoused, prevalent at the time, provided justification for inequities in the public school system.

In that commentary, we also remind readers that "vocational tracks prepared immigrants to be factory workers, while the children of well-off parents were given a college preparatory education. This pattern of separating students into different classes was repeated during the era of racial desegregation as a way to maintain segregated classrooms, and it was repeated again in the 1970s when students with special needs were increasingly enrolled in mainstream schools."[42]

The reemergence of vocational education is not the only troubling sign. Tom Loveless, one of tracking's most ardent supporters, reported that ability grouping is on the rise in elementary schools, and he speculates that test-based accountability is partially responsible for the upswing: "Accountability systems, bolstered by the accountability provisions of No Child Left Behind, focus educators' attention on students below the threshold for 'proficiency' on state tests. That provides a statutory justification for grouping students who are struggling."[43] Loveless expands the definition of *ability grouping* to include flexible reading groups within the heterogeneous classroom, often referred to as "leveled reading." The traditional definition denotes entire classes grouped by ability. Although I differ with Loveless's inclusion of leveled reading groups within the heterogeneous class as ability grouping, his observation of an upswing in such grouping due to accountability measures is correct. The more that test scores reflecting student "growth" are emphasized in teacher evaluation, the more likely it is that teachers will isolate groups of students and drill them in an attempt to raise their scores.

Ironically, even as ability grouping regains some popularity, the most recent literature on the practice still does not support it, associating it with lower gains at the elementary level for lower-ability groups and no gains for any other group.[44] Using data from eighteen developed countries in Europe, North America, and Asia, Eric Hanushek and Ludger Woessmann found that early tracking increased inequitable learning outcomes while depressing overall student achievement.[45]

Despite these findings, there is little doubt that some teachers and principals, anxious over test scores, will continue to group students, especially high- and low-scoring students, in an attempt to push their growth to increase evaluation scores. When the "wrong drivers"—

punitive systems of evaluation and accountability—are used to implement reform, the wrong strategies often follow.[46]

And so we end this book where it began, with the boy with the purple tie. The school designed to meet his needs exists because of the belief, expressed by its headmaster, that streaming "is the only way to survive in the brave new world of market-driven education."[47] Such a view makes it likely that sort-and-select policies and practices will drive the reform agenda in the next decade, and data will continue to be used to funnel students into disparate life-stations. This century's captains of industry want the best return on their business and philanthropic investments, and this means that, as was the case at the turn of the last century, they will expect schools to deliver the variety of workers they desire, from engineers to auto mechanics. If the market-based reforms so in vogue hold sway, parental-choice systems and standardized test scores will be used to perpetuate the same stratification by class and race that led to separate and unequal education.

The stories in this book, however, give us hope in those who are standing up and fighting for what is best for *students*, not for business. Despite fierce opposition, educators who believe in the great potential of diverse, democratic classrooms and schools that challenge all children continue to make real progress. Yes, in instituting change they looked at test scores, but they were able to look beyond scores as well. They held fast to the belief that each child is unique and that a student's potential cannot be determined by objective measures alone. They believe that schools need to be socially as well as academically sound. They understand the impulse to sort and select, and how some students, already advantaged by life's circumstances, would reap further advantage at the expense of others.

Leaders of the democratic reform movement, including those described in this book, will continue to fight for equality of opportunity for *all* students. They will continue to reveal, and to push back against, the consequences—intended and unintended—of marketplace-driven initiatives that perpetuate inequities in our education system. These leaders understand that in our public schools, the playing field must be leveled, the doors of opportunity swung wide, and the supports that enable *all* students to succeed provided. Be they parents like Wendy Lecker, school board members like Mark Metz, or superintendents like Bill Johnson, these leaders will not abandon their beliefs. They will continue to advocate for all our students, to rise to the challenge of democratic school reform with patience and confidence, until every child gets to wear the purple tie.

Note from the Series Editor

The Simmons College/Beacon Press Race, Education, and Democracy Lecture and Book Series, a collaborative effort of Simmons College and Beacon Press, annually brings to Boston a prominent public figure to deliver public lectures on the topic of race, education, and democracy. These lectures form the basis for a book published each year by Beacon Press.

The series aims to reestablish in the public imagination the historic connection between public education and the possibility of a robust democracy, against the backdrop of the issue of race in America. It aims to create a location for a sustained, public conversation about the purpose of education in a multiracial and multicultural democracy. It aims to create a place for individuals to examine critically what should happen in school—if school is to prepare the young for the democracy, if school is to be the place where a new common culture, predicated on difference, is created and recreated. It aims to create a location for Americans to examine what is required of schools, the country, and the citizenry if the young are to be educated for self-government, when definitions of what is real, who is of value, and who are members of the nation are daily constructed and worked out in media.

Racial ideology continues to present a significant threat to Horace Mann's vision of public education as the great equalizer and to the belief of Frederick Douglass and other formerly enslaved Africans that education was indeed the pathway from slavery to freedom. The Simmons College/Beacon Press series seeks to help strengthen the relationship between education and the democracy, with a broader vision of who members of the democracy are, while unapologetically introducing race into this discourse.

The series is geared to a broad audience: educators, concerned citizens, parents, students, community activists, and civic, religious and business leaders. The lectures and books present educational issues in all their complexity, yet in a manner that is readily accessible to a wide audience. The series proceeds on the assumption that public education is at the center of American public life and that discussions about critical educational issues need to occur in the public sphere and draw Americans from many different backgrounds into thoughtful, informed, and complicated conversations.

We hope that these lectures and books will spark a new energy and excitement about education and the necessary role it must play in democratic life, and create a general audience of readers for critical educational scholarship.

THERESA PERRY
Series Director
Professor of Africana Studies
and Education
Simmons College
Boston

Notes

INTRODUCTION

1. See Jeannie Oakes, *Keeping Track: How Schools Structure Inequality* (New Haven, CT: Yale University Press, 1985).

I. THE BOY WITH THE PURPLE TIE

1. Rowenna Davis, "School Colour-Codes Pupils by Ability," *Guardian* (UK), July 25, 2011, http://www.theguardian.com/.
2. Ibid.
3. Samuel R. Lucas, *Tracking Inequality: Stratification and Mobility in American High Schools* (New York: Teachers College Press, 1999).
4. Jeannie Oakes, *Keeping Track: How Schools Structure Inequality* (New Haven, CT: Yale University Press, 1985).
5. Jeannie Oakes, *The Tracking Wars: The Struggle for Equity in Diverse Schools* (Philadelphia: Delaware Valley Minority Student Consortium, 2006).
6. Raymond E. Callahan, *Education and the Cult of Efficiency* (Chicago: University of Chicago Press, 1962).
7. See Oakes, *Keeping Track*.
8. See Joel H. Spring's *Education and the Rise of the Corporate State* (Boston: Beacon Press, 1972).
9. Ibid., 33.
10. See Herbert M. Kliebard, *The Struggle for the American Curriculum, 1893–1958*, 2nd ed. (New York: Routledge, 1995).

11. Kevin G. Welner, *Legal Rights, Local Wrongs: When Community Control Collides with Educational Equity* (Albany: State University of New York Press, 2001).

12. Talcott Parsons, "The School Class as a Social System: Some of Its Functions in American Society," *Harvard Educational Review* 29 (1959), 297–318.

13. Ibid.

14. See Karl L. Alexander and Edward L. McDill, *Selection and Allocation Within Schools: Some Causes and Consequences of Curriculum Placement*, Report No. 213 (Baltimore, MD: Johns Hopkins University, Center for Social Organization of Schools, 1976).

15. Ibid., 24.

16. Barbara Heyns and David K. Cohen, *Curriculum Assignment and Tracking Policies in Forty-Eight Urban Public High Schools, Final Report* (Washington, DC: Center for Education Policy Research, 1971).

17. Barbara Heyns, "Social Selection and Stratification Within Schools," *American Journal of Sociology* 79, no. 6 (1974): 1434–51.

18. Alexander and McDill, *Selection and Allocation Within Schools*, 75.

19. James E. Rosenbaum, "Track Misperceptions and Frustrated College Plans: An Analysis of the Effects of Tracks and Track Perceptions in the National Longitudinal Survey," *Sociology of Education* 53 (1990): 76.

20. See Welner, *Legal Rights, Local Wrongs*.

21. Hobson v. Hansen, 269 F.Supp. 401 (D.D.C. 1967). See Em Hall, "On the Road to Educational Failure: A Lawyer's Guide to Tracking," *Inequality in Education* 5 (Cambridge, MA: Harvard Center for Law and Education, 1970).

22. Hall, "On the Road to Educational Failure," 4.

23. Ibid., 1.

24. *Fulfilling the Letter and Spirit of the Law: Desegregation of the Nation's Public Schools* (Washington, DC: US Commission on Civil Rights, 1976).

25. Ibid.

26. Janet Eyler et al., "Resegregation: Segregation Within Desegregated Schools," in *Assessment of Current Knowledge About the Effectiveness of School Desegregation Strategies*, vol. 5, *A Review of the Empirical Research on Desegregation: Community Response, Race Relations, Academic Achievement and Resegregation*, ed. W. D. Hawley (Nashville, TN: Van-

derbilt University, Institute for Public Policy Studies, Center for Education and Human Development Policy, 1981).

27. Jeannie Oakes, "Tracking and Educational Equity: Curricular Content,
Instructional Practice, and Social Relationships in 156 Secondary English Classes" (PhD diss., University of California, Los Angeles, 1980).

2. KEEPING TRACK

1. Jeannie Oakes was most generous with her time when I interviewed her
for this chapter during the summer of 2012.

2. John Goodlad, *A Placed Called School: Prospects for the Future* (New
York: McGraw-Hill, 1984).

3. Jeannie Oakes, "Tracking and Inequality Within Schools: Findings
from a Study of Schooling," paper presented at the Annual Meeting
of the American Education Research Association, Boston, April 7–11,
1980.

4. Jeannie Oakes, *Keeping Track: How Schools Structure Inequality* (New
Haven, CT: Yale University Press, 1985).

5. Ibid., 68–71.

6. Oakes, "Tracking and Inequality Within Schools," 42–43.

7. Merrilee Finley, "Teachers and Tracking in a Comprehensive High
School," *Sociology of Education* 57, no. 4 (1984): 233–43.

8. Donald J. Veldman and Julie P. Sanford, "The Influence of Class Ability Level on Student Achievement and Classroom Behavior," *American
Educational Research Journal* 21, no. 3 (Autumn 1984): 629–44.

9. Karl L. Alexander and Edward L. McDill, *Selection and Allocation Within
Schools: Some Causes and Consequences of Curriculum Placement*, Report
No. 213 (Baltimore: Johns Hopkins University, Center for Social Orga-
nization of Schools, 1976).

10. National Education Association, "Ability Grouping: Teacher Opinion
Poll," *NEA Journal* 57 (1968): 53.

11. Jay P. Heubert and Robert M. Hauser, eds., *High Stakes: Testing for Tracking, Promotion, and Graduation* (Washington, DC: National Academy
Press, 1999).

12. Oakes, *Keeping Track*.

13. Hobson v. Hansen, 269 F. Supp. 401 (D.D.C. 1967) at 515.

14. Jeannie Oakes, "Tracking and Ability Grouping in American Schools: Some Constitutional Questions." Paper presented at the Annual Meeting of the American Educational Research Association, Los Angeles, April 13–17, 1981.

15. See Kevin G. Welner, *Legal Rights, Local Wrongs: When Community Control Collides with Educational Equity* (Albany: State University of New York Press, 2001).

16. Oakes, "Tracking and Ability Grouping in American Schools."

17. *Fulfilling the Letter and Spirit of the Law: Desegregation of the Nation's Public Schools* (Washington, DC: US Commission on Civil Rights, 1976), 234.

18. Ibid., 237.

19. See John Rose Jr. et al., *School Desegregation in Stamford, Connecticut: A Report Prepared by the Connecticut Advisory Committee to the US Commission on Civil Rights* (Washington, DC: US Commission on Civil Rights, 1977).

20. Ibid., 35.

21. This stratified system would remain in place for the next thirty years, until Superintendent Josh Starr reduced the number of tracks in the middle school. Chapter 7 includes an extensive discussion of that process and its challenges.

22. Rose et al., *School Desegregation in Stamford.*

23. Ibid., 37.

24. Ibid.

25. See Rebecca Barr and Robert Dreeben, *How Schools Work* (Chicago: University of Chicago Press, 1983).

3. TRACKING AND CLASSROOM SEGREGATION

1. See, for example, Robert E. Slavin, "Achievement Effects of Ability Grouping in Secondary Schools: A Best-Evidence Synthesis," *Review of Educational Research* 60, no. 3 (1990): 471–99.

2. The report that resulted from the study is Oakes et al., *Multiplying Inequalities: The Effects of Race, Social Class, and Tracking on Opportunities to Learn Mathematics and Science* (Washington, DC: National Science Foundation, 1990).

3. Gatekeeper courses are prerequisites for advanced placement; acceler-

ated algebra is called a gatekeeper course because it allows students to move on to calculus by grade twelve.

4. For the extensive body of research on this topic see, among others, Susan Black, "On the Wrong Track," *Executive Educator* 14, no. 12 (1992): 46–49; Jomills H. Braddock II and Marvin P. Dawkins, "Ability Grouping, Aspirations, and Attainments: Evidence from the National Educational Longitudinal Study of 1988," *Journal of Negro Education* 62, no. 3 (1993): 324–36; Oakes et al., *Multiplying Inequalities.*

5. See Samuel R. Lucas, *Tracking Inequality: Stratification and Mobility in American High Schools* (New York: Teachers College Press, 1999); Samuel R. Lucas and Adam Gamoran, *Race and Track Assignment: A Reconsideration with Course-Based Indicators of Track Locations* (Washington, DC: Office of Educational Research and Improvement, 1993); Beth E. Vanfossen et al., "Curriculum Tracking and Status Maintenance," *Sociology of Education* 60, no. 2 (1987): 104–22.

6. Vanfossen et al., "Curriculum Tracking and Status Maintenance."

7. See Lucas and Gamoran, *Race and Track Assignment*; Oakes et al., *Multiplying Inequalities.*

8. Jeannie Oakes, "Keeping Track, Part 1: The Policy and Practice of Curriculum Inequality," *Phi Delta Kappan* 68 (1986): 12–18.

9. For an example of this argument, see Tom Loveless, "Will Tracking Promote Social Equity?" *Educational Leadership* 56, no. 7 (1999): 28–32.

10. Lucas and Gamoran, *Race and Track Assignment.*

11. Kevin Welner is a prominent scholar of equity issues and educational policy. He currently serves as director of the National Educational Policy Center at the University of Colorado at Boulder, where he is also a professor of education policy. The discussion in this chapter is based on phone interviews I conducted with Welner and with Jeannie Oakes in August 2012, as well as Welner's *Legal Rights, Local Wrongs: When Community Control Collides with Educational Equity* (Albany: State University of New York Press, 2001).

12. See Welner, *Legal Rights, Local Wrongs.*

13. Ibid., 82.

14. See Edward Kifer, "Opportunities, Talents and Participation," in *The IEA Study of Mathematics III: Student Growth and Classroom Processes,* Leigh Burstein, ed. (Oxford, UK: Pergamon Press, 1993), 279–308.

15. See Elizabeth L. Useem, "Getting on the Fast Track in Mathematics: School Organizational Influences on Math Track Assignment," *American Journal of Education* 100, no. 3 (1992), 325–53; Elizabeth L. Useem, "Middle Schools and Math Groups: Parents' Involvement in Children's Placement," *Sociology of Education* 65, no. 4 (1992): 263–79.

16. See Annette Lareau, *Home Advantage: Social Class and Parental Intervention in Elementary Education* (Philadelphia: Falmer Press, 1989).

17. Susan Yonezawa et al., "Choosing Tracks: 'Freedom of Choice' in Detracking Schools," *American Educational Research Journal* 39, no. 1 (2002): 37–67.

18. Ibid., 60.

19. Capers et al. v. Board of Education of the City School District of the City of New York (2013). This complaint, prepared by attorney Wendy Lecker, was filed with the US Department of Education Office for Civil Rights.

20. The table is based on New York State Department of Education data, available at www.nysed.gov.

21. For a discussion of the entrance exam, its use and its limitations, see Joshua Feinman, *High Stakes but Low Validity? A Case Study of Standardized Tests and Admissions into New York City's Specialized High Schools* (Boulder, CO: National Education Policy Center, 2008), http://nepc .colorado.edu/.

22. See Jennifer Medina, "At Top City Schools, Lack of Diversity Persists," February 5, 2010, *City Room* blog, *New York Times*, http://cityroom.blogs .nytimes.com/.

23. Feinman, *High Stakes but Low Validity?*

24. See Jay Mathews, "Diversity Lags at Highly Selective Thomas Jefferson High School," *Class Struggle* blog, June 10, 2012, *Washington Post*, http:// www.washingtonpost.com/blogs/class-struggle/.

25. See Jonathan Allen, "NAACP to File Complaint Alleging Bias at New York City High Schools," September 26, 2012, *Huffington Post*, http:// www.huffingtonpost.com/.

26. Michael Becker et al., "The Differential Effects of School Tracking on Psychometric Intelligence: Do Academic-Track Schools Make Students Smarter?" *Journal of Educational Psychology* 104, no. 3 (2012): 682–99.

4. TRACKING AND STUDENT ACHIEVEMENT

1. See Robert E. Slavin, "Achievement Effects of Ability Grouping in Secondary Schools: A Best-Evidence Synthesis," *Review of Educational Research* 60, no. 3 (1990): 471–99.

2. Ibid., 485.

3. See Chen-Lin C. Kulik and James A. Kulik, "Effects of Ability Grouping on Secondary School Students: A Meta-Analysis of Evaluation Findings," *American Educational Research Journal* 19, no. 3 (1982): 415–28.

4. See Ning Rui, "Four Decades of Research on the Effects of Detracking Reform: Where Do We Stand?—A Systemic Review of the Evidence," *Journal of Evidence Based Medicine* 2, no. 3 (2009): 164–83.

5. Karl L. Alexander and Martha A. Cook, "Curricula and Coursework: A Surprise Ending to a Familiar Story," *American Sociological Review* 47, no. 5 (1982): 626–40.

6. The 1980 High School and Beyond Survey utilized data collected by the National Center for Educational Statistics from a national sample of high school students.

7. Adam Gamoran, "The Stratification of High School Learning Opportunities," *Sociology of Education* 60, no. 3 (1987): 135–55.

8. See Beth E. Vanfossen et al., "Curriculum Tracking and Status Maintenance," *Sociology of Education* 60 (1987): 104–22; Thomas B. Hoffer, "Middle School Ability Grouping and Student Achievement in Science and Mathematics," *Educational Evaluation and Policy Analysis* 14, no. 3 (1992): 205–27; Ginger N. Goff, "Assessing the Impact of Tracking on Individual Growth in Mathematics Achievement Using Random Coefficient Modeling," *Dissertation Abstracts International* 56, no. 3 (1995): 855 (University Microfilms no. 9523572).

9. Alan C. Kerckhoff, "Effects of Ability Grouping in British Secondary Schools," *American Sociological Review* 51, no. 6 (1986): 842–58.

10. See the following two articles for a synopsis of the Brewer studies: Dominic J. Brewer, "Detracking America's Schools: The Reform Without Cost?" *Phi Delta Kappan* 77, no. 6 (1995): 210; Dominic J. Brewer et al., "The Reform Without Costs? A Reply to Our Critics," *Phi Delta Kappan* 77, no. 6 (1996): 442–44.

11. See Tom Loveless, *The Tracking Wars: State Reform Meets School Policy* (Washington, DC: Brookings Institution Press, 1999); "Will Tracking

Reform Promote Social Equity?" *Educational Leadership* 56, no. 7 (1999): 28–32.

12. Samuel R. Lucas and Adam Gamoran, *Race and Track Assignment: A Reconsideration with Course-Based Indicators of Track Locations* (Washington, DC: Office of Educational Research and Improvement, 1993). See also chapter 1 for discussion of the 1980 findings by Rosenbaum.

13. See Richard M. Jaeger and John A. Hattie, "Detracking America's Schools: Should We Really Care?" *Phi Delta Kappan* 77 (1995): 218-19; Robert E. Slavin, "Detracking and Its Detractors: Flawed Evidence, Flawed Values," *Phi Delta Kappan* 77 (1995): 220–21.

14. See Jay P. Hubert and Robert M. Hauser, eds., *High Stakes: Testing for Tracking, Promotion, and Graduation* (Washington, DC: National Academy Press, 1999).

15. See James A. Kulik, *An Analysis of the Research on Ability Grouping: Historical and Contemporary Perspectives* (Storrs, CT: National Research Center on the Gifted and Talented, 1992).

16. See Christine Finnan and Julie D. Swanson, *Accelerating the Learning of All Students: Cultivating Culture Change in Schools, Classrooms, and Individuals* (Boulder, CO: Westview Press, 2000); Henry M. Levin, *Accelerated Schools for At-Risk Students*, CPRE Research Report No. 142 (Philadelphia: Consortium for Policy Research in Education, 1988).

17. DeWayne A. Mason et al., "Assigning Average-Achieving Eighth Graders to Advanced Mathematics Classes in an Urban Junior High," *Elementary School Journal* 92, no. 5 (1992): 587–99.

18. Howard S. Bloom et al., *Evaluating the Accelerated Schools Approach: A Look at Early Implementation and Impacts on Student Achievement in Eight Elementary Schools* (New York: Manpower Demonstration Research Corporation, 2001).

19. John M. Peterson, "Remediation Is No Remedy," *Educational Leadership* 46, no. 6 (1989): 24–25.

20. See Paula A. White et al., "Upgrading the High School Math Curriculum: Math Course-Taking Patterns in Seven High Schools in California and New York," *Educational Evaluation and Policy Analysis* 18, no. 4 (1996): 285–307.

21. Liora Linchevski and Bilha Kutscher, "Tell Me With Whom You're Learning, and I'll Tell You How Much You've Learned: Mixed-Ability

Versus Same-Ability Grouping in Mathematics," *Journal for Research in Mathematics Education* 29, no. 5 (1998): 533–54.

22. Carol Corbett Burris et al., "A World-Class Curriculum for All," *Educational Leadership* 64, no. 7 (2007): 53–56; Carol Corbett Burris et al., "Accountability, Rigor, and Detracking: Achievement Effects of Embracing a Challenging Curriculum as a Universal Good for All Students," *Teachers College Record* 110, no. 3 (2008): 571–608.

23. The results of studies that measured those effects are reported in Carol Corbett Burris and Kevin G. Welner, "Closing the Achievement Gap by Detracking," *Phi Delta Kappan* 86, no. 8 (2005): 594–98; Carol Corbett Burris et al., "A World-Class Curriculum for All"; Carol Corbett Burris et al., "Accountability, Rigor, and Detracking."

5. THE DISTRICT THAT STOPPED SORTING STUDENTS

1. Dr. Bill Johnson generously shared his time with me during the fall of 2012. The information in this chapter comes from that interview, as well as my own research and recollection of events.

2. I interviewed Larry Vandewater in 1999 for my doctoral work at Teachers College; during that interview he shared with me his philosophy of middle school.

3. New York State required schools to provide highly proficient math students with the opportunity to take algebra, normally a ninth-grade course, in the eighth grade. If the school were to detrack math, it had to provide that opportunity to all students.

4. Information regarding changes to instruction and the process of implementation were provided to me by Delia Garrity, the former assistant principal and assistant superintendent for curriculum and instruction of the Rockville Centre School District, during an interview in 2002.

5. For a summary of this initiative, along with the long-term results for students in three consecutive cohorts, see Carol Burris, Jay P. Heubert, and Henry M. Levin, "Accelerating Mathematics Achievement Using Heterogeneous Grouping," *American Educational Research Journal* 43, no. 1 (2006): 103–34.

6. Despite changes in regulations and an easing of diploma requirements, the state continues to revise the date for the elimination of the local diploma, at least for special education, Section 504, and declassified students.

7. International Baccalaureate Organization, *Diploma Programme Assessment: Principles and Practice* (Cardiff, Wales, UK: International Baccalaureate Organization, 2004), http://web3.ibo.org/ibis/documents/dp/d_x_dpyyy_ass_0409_1_e.pdf.

8. See Kevin Welner and Carol C. Burris, "Alternative Approaches to the Politics of Detracking," *Theory into Practice* 45, no. 1 (2006): 90–99.

6. THE POLITICS OF DETRACKING

1. See Jeannie Oakes et al., "Detracking: The Social Construction of Ability, Cultural Politics, and Resistance to Reform," *Teachers College Record* 98, no. 3 (1997): 482–510.

2. Kevin Welner, *Legal Rights, Local Wrongs: When Community Control Collides with Educational Equity* (Albany: State University of New York Press, 2001).

3. Oakes et al., "Detracking."

4. For a description of the research on the multiple intelligences of children, see Howard Gardner, *Multiple Intelligences: The Theory in Practice* (New York: Basic Books, 1993).

5. Oakes et al., "Detracking."

6. The detracking process at this school is described in more detail in a later chapter. The school administrator who related this story to me wished to remain anonymous; other sources involved confirmed its veracity.

7. See Welner, *Legal Rights, Local Wrongs*.

8. See Beth C. Rubin, "Detracking in Context: How Local Constructions of Ability Complicate Equity-Geared Reform," *Teachers College Record* 110, no. 3 (2008): 646–99.

9. Ibid., 681.

10. Based on interviews with the principal of what will be referred to in a later chapter as New England High School. The principal wished to re-

main anonymous. Statements and descriptions were confirmed by additional interviews and a site visit.

11. Jeannie Oakes and Martin Lipton, "Struggling for Educational Equity in Diverse Communities: School Reform as Social Movement," *Journal of Educational Change* 3, nos. 3–4 (2002): 383–406.

12. Ibid., 390.

13. See Welner, *Legal Rights, Local Wrongs.*

14. Researchers such as Tom Loveless often make the case that "reformed" tracking systems are equitable. See, for example, *The Tracking and Ability Grouping Debate* (Washington, DC: Thomas B. Fordham Institute, 1998), www.edexcellence.net/publications/tracking.html.

15. For the research, see Samuel R. Lucas, *Tracking Inequality: Stratification and Mobility in American High Schools* (New York: Teachers College Press, 1999).

16. See Paul Attewell, "The Winner-Take-All High School: Organizational Adaptations to Educational Stratification," *Sociology of Education* 74, no. 4 (2001): 267–95.

17. See Jeannie Oakes and Amy Stuart Wells, "Doing the Right Thing: The Struggle to 'Detrack' Secondary Schools," *California English* 2, no. 1 (1996): 11.

7. RACE AND DETRACKING

1. For a summary of what occurred, see background, Hoots v. Pennsylvania, 118 F.Supp.2d 577 (Dist. Court, W.D. Pa. 2000), *FindACase*, http://pa.findacase.com/.

2. I interviewed Dr. Stanley Herman in October 2012. He was most generous with his time. Most, although not all, of what follows is based on his recollections. In those instances where other sources are used, they are noted.

3. See Kevin G. Welner, "Tracking in an Era of Standards: Low-Expectation Classes Meet High-Expectation Laws," *Hastings Constitutional Law Quarterly* 28, no. 3 (2001): 699–738.

4. The court mandates regarding mathematics and how the district responded to those mandates can be found in the decision to give the dis-

trict full unitary status: Hoots v. Pennsylvania 118 F.Supp.2d 577 (W.D. Pa. 2000).

5. See Eleanor Chute, "Woodland Hills Balances Freedom Against Balanced Budget," *Pittsburgh Post-Gazette*, June 13, 2003, http://old.post -gazette.com/.

6. The current levels of course offerings and the "gifted" course catalog can be viewed on the Woodland Hills School District website: http://www1 .whsd.net/.

7. Data from the Pennsylvania Department of Education website, at "Data and Statistics," http://www.education.state.pa.us/.

8. In a July 2012 interview, Josh Starr generously shared with me his perspective on and recollections of the detracking efforts of the Stamford, Connecticut, schools. During an interview in the spring of 2012 and in subsequent emails, parent activist Wendy Lecker also shared with me her recollections and interpretation of events. Most of what follows, unless noted, is derived from those interviews.

9. A description of the desegregation plan can be found in *School Desegregation in Stamford, Connecticut, a Report Prepared by the Connecticut Advisory Committee to the US Commission on Civil Rights* (Washington, DC: US Commission on Civil Rights, 1977). This document also records the testimony given about ability grouping. The findings and recommendations on ability grouping can be found on page 62.

10. See *A Curriculum Management Audit of the Elementary Language Arts Program, Stamford Public Schools* (Bloomington, IN: Phi Delta Kappan International, 2009). The report is available on the website of the Stamford Public Schools, http://stamfordpublicschools.org/.

11. The post, attributed to "Antonio R," appeared on the Stamford School District's City-Data Forum: http://www.city-data.com/forum/ connecticut/789758-stamford-school-district.html.

12. Cindy Grafstein generously shared her wisdom and perspective with me in an interview in November 2012.

13. Data for the graph can be found at http://www.stamfordpublicschools .org/filestorage/64/2839/GE_Conference_July2208.pdf.

14. "Reforming Schools' Ability Grouping," editorial, *Stamford Advocate*, March 8, 2009.

15. See Winnie Hu, "No Longer Letting Scores Separate Pupils," *New York Times*, June 14, 2009, http://www.nytimes.com/.

16. See Gary Klein, "Another View Regarding Middle School Reform," *Stamford Advocate*, January 14, 2010, http://stamfordadvocate.com/.

17. Jackie Heftman shared her recollections with me in a telephone interview in November 2012.

18. See Joshua P. Starr, "Middle School Transformation Off to a Good Start, With More to Do," January 2010, available on the website of the Stamford Public Schools, http://stamfordpublicschools.org/.

19. Quoted in Marion Herbert, "Middle School Transformation Plan Will Continue—for Now," May 11, 2011, *Stamford Patch*, http://stamford.patch.com/.

20. See Maggie Gordon, "Jack Bryant: NAACP Will Sue If Tracking Returns to Stamford Schools," *Stamford Advocate*, April 28, 2011, http://www.stamfordadvocate.com/.

21. Maggie Gordon, "GE Threatens to Pull Funding over Tracking Students," *Stamford Advocate*, February 4, 2011, http://www.stamfordadvocate.com/.

22. See Paul George's informative booklet, *How to Untrack Your School* (Alexandria, VA: Association for Supervision and Curriculum Development, 1992).

8. TRACKING AND LEADERSHIP

1. Carol Corbett Burris and Delia T. Garrity, *Detracking for Excellence and Equity* (Alexandria, VA: Association for Supervision and Curriculum Development, 2008).

2. "Miriam Reynolds" is a pseudonym. Although the school principal was willing to be interviewed for this book, she wished to remain anonymous. Information she supplied about the school and its detracking reform was independently confirmed through other sources.

3. "Sullins High," "Bayhill Schools," and "Lyons Bay" are pseudonyms, as are all names for places and people discussed in this section. The story of Sullins is derived primarily from sources who wished to remain anonymous—school leaders and parents. Every anecdote was confirmed by at

least two sources. The primary source was the school principal. Minor details were altered to preserve anonymity.

4. Amy Stuart Wells and Jeannie Oakes, "Potential Pitfalls of Systemic Reform: Early Lessons from Research on Detracking," *Sociology of Education* 69, no. 2 (1996): 135–43.

5. I interviewed Mark Metz via telephone in the fall of 2012.

6. David Futransky is a fourteen-year veteran of the school who is active in promoting civic engagement. He graciously agreed to be interviewed by phone in the fall of 2012.

7. Information regarding the changes to the tracking system in 2008 is derived from interviews and Megan Crepeau, "Community Gives ETHS Feedback on Detracking Plan," *Daily Northwestern*, February 14, 2008.

8. Quoted in Crepeau, "Community Gives ETHS Feedback on Detracking Plan."

9. Ibid.

10. Quoted in Jennie Berkson, "District 202 Freshman Humanities Proposal Approved," *Evanston (IL) Roundtable*, March 19, 2008.

11. Quoted in Karen Berkowitz, "Detracking Stokes Debate," *Evanston Review*, November 20, 2008.

12. Quoted in Berkson, "District 202 Freshman Humanities Proposal Approved."

13. I interviewed Jennifer Fisher, a teacher in the district since 1978, during the fall of 2012.

14. I interviewed Associate Principal Marcus Campbell in the fall of 2012.

15. Diane Rado, "Evanston Township High School District 202 Eliminates Honors Humanities Course," *Chicago Tribune*, December 14, 2010.

16. Sofia Resnick, "Beyond the Bickering: A Deeper Look at ETHS' Curriculum Proposal," *Evanston Patch*, December 10, 2010.

17. Diane Rado, "Evanston Township High School District 202 Eliminates Honors Humanities Course."

18. "Honors? Horrors!" editorial, *Chicago Tribune*, December 17, 2010.

19. Northwestern University's athletic teams are the Wildcats, hence the name Wildkits.

20. Charles Bartling, "'Wait and See' Wins Out over 'Let's Do It Now,'" *Evanston Now*, December 11, 2012, http://evanstonnow.com.

21. See Paul George, *How to Untrack Your School* (Alexandria, VA: Association for Supervision and Curriculum Development, 1992); Amy Stuart Wells and Irene Serna, "The Politics of Culture: Understanding Local Political Resistance to Detracking in Racially Mixed Schools," *Harvard Educational Review* 66, no. 1 (1996): 93–118.

22. Delia Garrity and I present an extensive description of how a school can overcome the three P's in *Detracking for Excellence and Equity*. The data to be collected is also listed in that publication.

23. Quoted in Bartling, "'Wait and See' Wins Out over 'Let's Do It Now.'"

24. Jay P. Heubert and Robert M. Hauser, eds., *High Stakes: Testing for Tracking, Promotion, and Graduation* (Washington, DC: National Academy Press, 1999).

25. When I refer to the ineffectiveness of low-track classes, I am not including specially designed programs for students with severe developmental delays such as Down syndrome or severe forms of autism. Although we should mainstream our seriously disabled students as much as possible, it is important that their unique needs to acquire life skills and social skills be met, and that often requires a separate setting within the school.

9. LESSONS LEARNED AND THE REFORMS OF TODAY

1. See T. S. Wilson, "Negotiating Public and Private," in *Exploring the School Choice Universe: Evidence and Recommendations*, ed. Gary Miron et al. (Charlotte, NC: Information Age Publishing, 2012).

2. Kenneth Howe et al., "School Choice Crucible: A Case Study of Boulder Valley," *Phi Delta Kappan* 83, no. 2 (2001): 137–46.

3. Ibid., 145.

4. Scott Imberman et al., "Katrina's Children: A Natural Experiment in Peer Effects from Hurricane Evacuees," working paper, National Bureau of Economic Research, Cambridge, MA, 2009, available from the website of Texas A&M University, Department of Economics: http://econ web.tamu.edu.

5. Clara Hemphill and Kim Naur, *The New Marketplace: How Small-School Reforms and School Choice Have Reshaped New York City High Schools* (New York: Center for New York City Affairs, 2009), http://www.new

school.edu/milano/nycaffairs/documents/TheNewMarketplace_
Report.pdf.

6. New York City Department of Education, *NYC Secondary Reform Selected Analysis* (Boston: Parthenon Group, 2006), http://www.parthenon
.com.

7. New York State has a four-level test outcome system, with Level 1 representing the lowest scores (far below proficiency) and Level 4 representing
the scores well above proficiency.

8. New York City Department of Education, *Beat-the-Odds HS Update*
(Boston: Parthenon Group, 2008), http://roundtheinkwell.files.wordpress
.com/2013/06/exhibit-c-ocr.pdf.

9. See Sean Corcoran and Henry M. Levin, "School Choice and Competition in the New York City Schools," in *Education Reform in New York
City: Ambitious Change in the Nation's Most Complex School System*, ed.
Jennifer A. O'Day, Catherine S. Bitter, and Louis M. Gomez (Cambridge, MA: Harvard Education Press, 2011).

10. Jackie Bennett, *Programmed to Fail: The Parthenon Report and Closing
Schools*, March 9, 2011, Edwize.org.

11. Ibid.

12. I first saw Kati Haycock and her PowerPoint presentation at a conference
in 2000. Tom Sobol, who was the director of the doctoral program I was
attending at Teachers College, was skeptical of Ms. Haycock's presentation and the message that it sent. Tom's early critique of reform by test
scores was far more on target than I realized at the time.

13. Al Baker, "Charges of Bias in Admission Test Policy at Eight Elite Public High Schools," *New York Times*, September 27, 2012, http://www.ny
times.com.

14. See "A Portrait of Segregation in New York City's Schools," *New York
Times*, May 11, 2012, http://www.nytimes.com.

15. Capers et al. v. Board of Education of the City School District of the
City of New York, Administrative Class Complaint to the US Department of Education Office of Civil Rights, NY 73851922, May 20, 2013.

16. Ibid., 13.

17. Sandra Tan, "Stacking the Deck Against Buffalo's Six Failing Schools,"
Buffalo News, July 24, 2013, http://www.buffalonews.com.

18. Roslyn A. Mickelson et al., "School Choice and Segregation by Race,

Ethnicity, Class, and Achievement," in *Exploring the School Choice Universe: Evidence and Recommendations*, ed. Gary Miron et al. (Charlotte, NC: Information Age Publishing, 2012).

19. Kevin Welner, "The Bottom Line on Charter School Studies," *The Answer Sheet* blog, WashingtonPost.com, September 24, 2013, http://www.washingtonpost.com/blogs/answer-sheet/wp/2013/09/24/the-bottom-line-on-charter-school-studies.

20. Mickelson et al., *School Choice and Segregation by Race, Ethnicity, Class, and Achievement*.

21. Robert Bifulco and Helen F. Ladd, "School Choice, Racial Segregation, and Test-Score Gaps: Evidence from North Carolina's Charter School Program," *Journal of Policy Analysis and Management* 26, no. 1 (2007): 31–56; Sue Sturgis, *In North Carolina, Resegregation by Charter?* Institute for Southern Studies, 2013, available from http://www.southernstudies.org/2013/01/in-north-carolina-school-resegregation-by-charter.html.

22. Sturgis, *In North Carolina*.

23. Max Brantley, "Judge Keeps State in Desegregation Case; Rules Against Little Rock School District's Fight Against Charter Schools," *Arkansas Blog*, January 17, 2013, *Arkansas Times*, http://www.arktimes.com.

24. Ibid.

25. Jay Bookman, "State-Created Charter Schools Sidestep Public Schools," Jay Bookman blog, October 1, 2012, http://blogs.ajc.com/jay-bookman-blog.

26. See Natalie Lacireno-Paquet et al., "Creaming Versus Cropping: Charter School Enrollment Practices in Response to Market Incentives," *Educational Evaluation and Policy Analysis* 24, no. 2 (2002): 145–58.

27. Emma Brown, "DC Charter Schools Expel Students at Far Higher Rates Than Traditional Public Schools," *Washington Post*, January 5, 2013, http://www.washingtonpost.com.

28. Janice Ereth, Susan Gramling, and Andrea Bogie, *CEO Leadership Academy: Programmatic Profile and Educational Performance, 2011–12 School Year* (Madison, WI: Children's Research Center, 2012).

29. Michael J. Petrilli, "The Charter Expulsion Flap," *Flypaper*, January 8, 2013, Thomas B. Fordham Institute, http://www.edexcellence.net.

30. "How Cookie-Cutter School Reforms Cement Class, Race Divisions," blog entry by Natalie Hopkinson in Valerie Strauss, *Answer Sheet*,

June 10, 2013, *Washington Post*, http://www.washingtonpost.com/blogs/answer-sheet/.

31. See Steven G. Rivkin et al., "Teachers, Schools, and Academic Achievement," *Econometrica* 73, no. 2 (2005): 417–58.

32. For more information, see "Race to the Top," http://www.whitehouse.gov/issues/education/k-12/race-to-the-top.

33. Ben Chapman and Tina Moore, "Teachers Call Release of Rankings a 'Witch Hunt,' Inaccurate," *New York Daily News*, February 25, 2012, http://www.nydailynews.com.

34. Derek Briggs and Ben Dominique, "Due Diligence and the Evaluation of Teachers," National Educational Policy Center, February 8, 2011, http://nepc.colorado.edu/.

35. See John J. Papay, "Different Tests, Different Answers: The Stability of Teacher Value-Added Estimates Across Outcome Measures," *American Educational Research Journal* 48, no. 1 (2011): 163–93; Daniel F. McCaffrey et al., *Evaluating Value-Added Models of Teacher Accountability* (Santa Monica, CA: RAND Corporation, 2004).

36. New York State Education Department, *2010–11 Beta Growth Model for Educator Evaluation Technical Report* (Washington, DC: American Institutes for Research, 2011). Available from the website of the New York State Education Department: http://www.nysed.gov.

37. Last spring, I received several resumes from New York City ELL teachers anxious to teach in the suburbs; they noted on their cover letters that they'd been rated "highly effective" teachers by student scores.

38. C. Kirabo Jackson, "Teacher Quality at the High-School Level: The Importance of Accounting for Tracks" (NBER Working Paper No. 17722, National Bureau of Economic Research, Cambridge, MA, 2012).

39. Ibid., 5.

40. Douglass Harris and Andrew A. Anderson, "Bias of Public Sector Worker Performance Monitoring: Theory and Empirical Evidence from Middle School Teachers," paper presented at the APPAM Fall Research Conference, Baltimore, November 10, 2012. Summary of findings available from the website of the Association for Public Policy Analysis and Management, www.apam.org.

41. News Corporation press release, June 28, 2012, www.newscorp.com/news/news_464.html.

42. Kevin Welner and Carol Burris, "Is American Education on a Bad Track?" *Albany Times Union*, June 7, 2013, http://www.timesunion.com.

43. Tom Loveless, *The Resurgence of Ability Grouping and Persistence of Tracking*, part 2 of the 2013 Brown Center Report on American Education (March 2013), available from the Brookings Institution, http://www.brookings.edu/.

44. See Christy Lleras and Claudia Rangel, "Ability Grouping Practices in Elementary School and African American/Hispanic Achievement," *American Journal of Education* 115 (February 2009): 279–304; Suzanne Macqueen, "Academic Outcomes from Between-Class Achievement Grouping: The Australian Primary Context," *Australian Educational Research* 39 (February 2012): 59–73.

45. Eric A. Hanushek and Ludger Woesmann, "Does Educational Tracking Affect Performance and Inequality? Differences-in-Differences Evidence Across Countries," *Economic Journal* 116 (2006): 63–76.

46. See Michael Fullan, "Choosing the Wrong Drivers for Whole System Reform," 2011, available from *Michael Fullan: Motion Leadership*, http://www.michaelfullan.com/media/13501655630.pdf.

47. Rowenna Davis, "School Colour-Codes Pupils by Ability," *Guardian* (UK), July 25, 2011, http://www.theguardian.com.

Index

Page numbers followed by an *f* or a *t* indicate a figure or table, respectively.